Contents

MW01131125

Scope & Sequence

Week 1	Initial, Medial, and Final Consonants: *b, f, r, k, m, p, d, l, n*		**Week 16**	Long *i* Vowel Patterns: *ie, igh*
Week 2	Initial, Medial, and Final Consonants: *s, t, v, h, w, j, y, q, x, z*		**Week 17**	Long *o* Vowel Digraphs: *oa, ow, oe*
Week 3	Short Vowel Sounds: *a, e, i, o, u*		**Week 18**	Long *u* Vowel Digraphs: *ue, ew, ui*
Week 4	CVC Words		**Week 19**	R-Controlled Vowels: *ar*, or, er, ir*, ur, air*, are*, ear**
Week 5	Long Vowel Sounds: *a, e, i, o, u*		**Week 20**	The Sounds of *oo**
Week 6	CVCe Words		**Week 21**	Short Vowel Digraphs: *ea, ou, ui*
Week 7	Long Vowel Sounds of *y*		**Week 22**	Variant Vowel Digraphs: *au, aw, al*
Week 8	Hard and Soft *c* and *g*		**Week 23**	Diphthongs: *ou, ow, oi, oy*
Week 9	Initial Consonant Blends with *s, r,* or *l*		**Week 24**	Syllabication
Week 10	Final Consonant Blends with *t, d, p,* or *k*		**Week 25**	The Schwa Sound
Week 11	Initial and Final Consonant Digraphs: *ch, sh*, th, wh**		**Week 26**	Silent Consonants: *k, w, b, h, t, l*
Week 12	Initial, Medial, and Final Consonant Digraphs: *ck, ng, ph, gh*		**Week 27**	Plural Noun Endings: *s, es, ves, ies*
			Week 28	Irregular Plural Nouns
Week 13	Variant Spellings of Consonant Sounds: *tch, dge*		**Week 29**	Inflectional Verb Endings: *-ed, -ing, -s, -es*
Week 14	Long *a* Vowel Digraphs: *ai, ay*		**Week 30**	Contractions
			Week 31	Prefixes: *re-, un-, mis-, dis-*
Week 15	Long *e* Vowel Digraphs: *ee, ea, ey, ie*		**Week 32**	Suffixes: *-ful, -less, -ly, -er, -or, -ness*

*Nontransferable sound in Spanish

Daily Phonics • EMC 2790 • © Evan-Moor Corp.

How to Use This Book

Daily Phonics provides systematic phonics instruction, practice, and application for students reading below grade level. Each week focuses on a phonics skill typically mastered in grade 1, 2, or 3. Daily lessons progress through scaffolded listening and speaking activities to writing and reading activities.

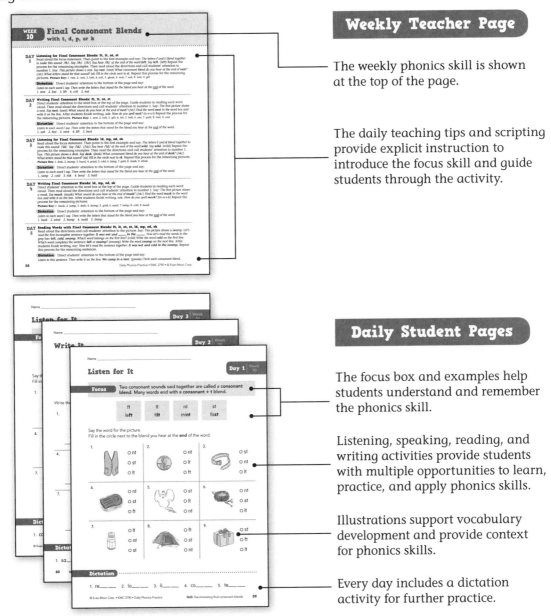

Weekly Teacher Page

The weekly phonics skill is shown at the top of the page.

The daily teaching tips and scripting provide explicit instruction to introduce the focus skill and guide students through the activity.

Daily Student Pages

The focus box and examples help students understand and remember the phonics skill.

Listening, speaking, reading, and writing activities provide students with multiple opportunities to learn, practice, and apply phonics skills.

Illustrations support vocabulary development and provide context for phonics skills.

Every day includes a dictation activity for further practice.

Working with English Language Learners

Pronunciation Is Key	Model how to pronounce letter-sounds and word chunks. Have students watch your mouth as you say a word. Then have students repeat the word.
Connect to Home Language	Be aware of nontransferable sounds and symbols in students' home languages. Help students articulate sounds in English that are new to them. Make connections to words in their home language.
Support Vocabulary Development	Develop vocabulary by connecting words to actions and providing context. Help students draw on background knowledge to connect vocabulary words to objects, concepts, actions, and situations they are familiar with.

Initial, Medial, and Final Consonants
b, f, r, k, m, p, d, l, n

DAY 1

Listening for Initial and Final Consonants: b, f, r

Read aloud the focus statement and point to each letter as you introduce its letter-sound. Say: *This is the letter b. The letter b is a consonant. It stands for this sound: /b/. Say /b/. (/b/) You hear the /b/ sound at the beginning of bat. Say bat. (bat) You hear /b/ at the end of tub. Say tub. (tub)* Repeat the process for the letters **f** and **r**. Then read the directions and call students' attention to number 1. Say: *Say bell.* (bell) *Do you hear /b/ first or last in bell?* (first) *Fill in the first circle.* Repeat the process for the remaining pictures.

Picture Key: 1. bell, 2. cab, 3. basket, 4. fan, 5. fish, 6. roof, 7. rocket, 8. star, 9. four

Dictation Direct students' attention to the bottom of the page. Say:

(for numbers 1–3) *Write the letter that stands for the first sound you hear in _____.*   1. bun   2. fin   3. ran

(for numbers 4–6) *Write the letter that stands for the last sound you hear in _____.*   4. tub   5. golf   6. car

DAY 2

Listening for Initial and Final Consonants: k, m, p

Read aloud the focus statement and point to each letter as you introduce its letter-sound. Say: *This is the letter k. The letter k is a consonant. It stands for this sound: /k/. Say /k/. (/k/) You hear the /k/ sound at the beginning of kite. Say kite. (kite) You hear the /k/ sound at the end of hook. Say hook. (hook)* Repeat the process for the letters **m** and **p**. Then read the directions and call students' attention to number 1. Say: *Say key.* (key) *Do you hear /k/ first or last in key?* (first) *Fill in the first circle.* Repeat the process for the remaining pictures.

Picture Key: 1. key, 2. duck, 3. book, 4. broom, 5. moose, 6. mitten, 7. purse, 8. jeep, 9. paint

Dictation Direct students' attention to the bottom of the page. Say:

(for numbers 1–3) *Write the letter that stands for the first sound you hear in _____.*   1. key   2. moon   3. pan

(for numbers 4–6) *Write the letter that stands for the last sound you hear in _____.*   4. book   5. gum   6. dip

DAY 3

Listening for Initial and Final Consonants: d, l, n

Read aloud the focus statement and point to each letter as you introduce its letter-sound. Say: *This is the letter d. The letter d is a consonant. It stands for this sound: /d/. Say /d/. (/d/) You hear the /d/ sound at the beginning of door. Say door. (door) You hear the /d/ sound at the end of cloud. Say cloud. (cloud)* Repeat the process for the letters **l** and **n**. Then read the directions and call students' attention to number 1. Ask: *Do you hear /d/ first or last in dog?* (first) *Fill in the first circle.* Repeat the process for the remaining pictures.

Picture Key: 1. dog, 2. dollar, 3. toad, 4. lamp, 5. school, 6. camel, 7. nest, 8. lion, 9. net

Dictation Direct students' attention to the bottom of the page. Say:

(for numbers 1–3) *Write the letter that stands for the first sound you hear in _____.*   1. dog   2. lip   3. net

(for numbers 4–6) *Write the letter that stands for the last sound you hear in _____.*   4. sad   5. seal   6. tan

DAY 4

Listening for Initial, Medial, and Final Consonants: b, f, r, k, m, p, d, l, n

Read aloud the focus statement. Then point to the example as you say: *The word medal has a consonant at the beginning, in the middle, and at the end. Say medal. (medal) What consonant sound do you hear in the middle? (/d/)* Then read aloud the directions and call students' attention to number 1. Say: *Point to the picture of a robot. What letters are below it? (b) What sound does the letter b have? (/b/) Say robot. (robot) Do you hear /b/ first, last, or in the middle? (middle) Circle the middle b.* Repeat the process for the remaining pictures and letters.

Picture Key: 1. robot, 2. kite, 3. lemon, 4. ship, 5. ladder, 6. leaf, 7. zipper, 8. jacket, 9. ham, 10. peanut, 11. ruler, 12. barrel

Dictation Direct students' attention to the bottom of the page and say:

Write the letter that stands for the middle sound you hear in _____.   1. lemon   2. robot   3. peanut   4. ruler

DAY 5

Writing Initial, Medial, and Final Consonants: b, f, r, k, m, p, d, l, n

Read aloud the directions and call students' attention to number 1. Say: *Say fan. (fan) What is the first sound in fan? (/f/) What letter stands for that sound? (f) Write f on the line.* Repeat the process for the remaining pictures.

Picture Key: 1. fan, 2. door, 3. robot, 4. rat, 5. cook, 6. ruler, 7. duck, 8. drum, 9. peanut, 10. pen, 11. toad, 12. paper

Dictation Direct students' attention to the bottom of the page and say:

(for numbers 1, 2) *Write the letter that stands for the first sound you hear in _____.*   1. log   2. rip

(for numbers 3, 4) *Write the letter that stands for the middle sound you hear in _____.*   3. cabin   4. menu

(for numbers 5, 6) *Write the letter that stands for the last sound you hear in _____.*   5. pan   6. bad

Name _____

Listen for It

Focus The letters **b**, **f**, and **r** are consonants. Each consonant has a different sound. Words may begin or end with a **b**, an **f**, or an **r**.

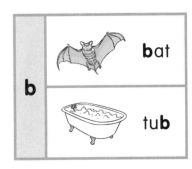
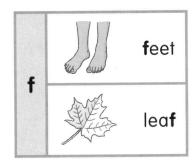
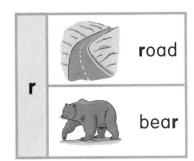

b — **b**at, tu**b**   **f** — **f**eet, lea**f**   **r** — **r**oad, bea**r**

Say the sound of the letter. Then say the word for the picture.
Fill in the circle to show if you hear the letter-sound **first** or **last**.

1. **b** ○——○

2.  **b** ○——○

3. **b** ○——○

4. **f** ○——○

5. **f** ○——○

6. 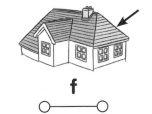 **f** ○——○

7.  **r** ○——○

8. **r** ○——○

9. **r** ○——○

Dictation •••

1. ___un   2. ___in   3. ___an   4. tu___   5. gol___   6. ca___

Skill: Discriminating initial and final consonants   **5**

Listen for It

Focus The letters **k**, **m**, and **p** are consonants. Each consonant has a sound. Words may begin or end with a **k**, an **m**, or a **p**.

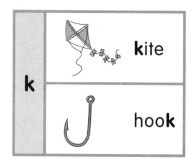

k — **k**ite / hoo**k**

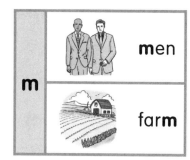

m — **m**en / far**m**

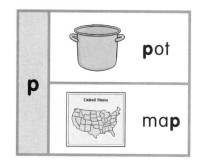

p — **p**ot / ma**p**

Say the sound of the letter. Then say the word for the picture.
Fill in the circle to show if you hear the letter-sound **first** or **last**.

1.

k
○——○

2.

k
○——○

3.

k
○——○

4.

m
○——○

5.

m
○——○

6.

m
○——○

7.

p
○——○

8.

p
○——○

9.

p
○——○

Dictation •

1. ___ey   2. ___oon   3. ___an   4. boo___   5. gu___   6. di___

Listen for It

Focus — The letters **d**, **l**, and **n** are consonants. Each consonant has a sound. Words may begin or end with a **d**, an **l**, or an **n**.

d	
	**d**oor
	clou**d**

l	
	**l**og
	nai**l**

n	
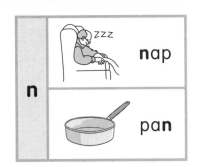	**n**ap
	pa**n**

Say the sound of the letter. Then say the word for the picture.
Fill in the circle to show if you hear the letter-sound **first** or **last**.

1.
d
○———○

2.
d
○———○

3.
d
○———○

4.
l
○———○

5.
l
○———○

6.
l
○———○

7.
n
○———○

8.
n
○———○

9.
n
○———○

Dictation ••

1. ___og   2. ___ip   3. ___et   4. sa___   5. sea___   6. ta___

Listen for It

| Focus | A word can begin or end with a consonant. A word can also have a consonant in the **middle**. |

Say the sound of the letter. Then say the word for the picture.
Circle the **first**, **middle**, or **last** letter to show where you hear the letter-sound.

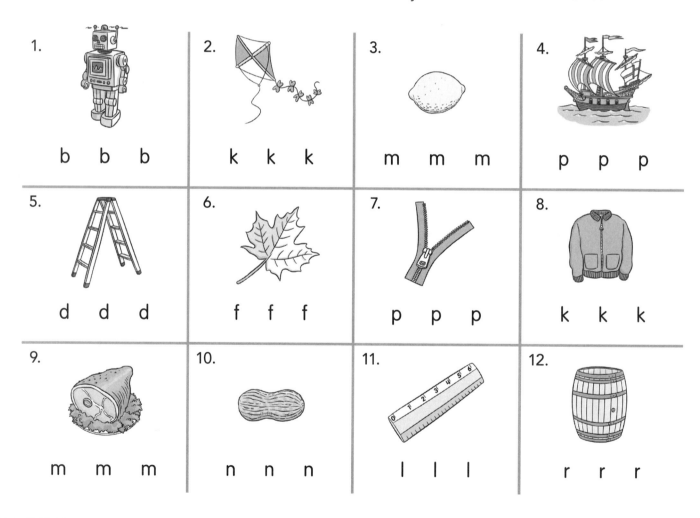

1.   b   b   b

2.   k   k   k

3.   m   m   m

4.   p   p   p

5.   d   d   d

6.   f   f   f

7.   p   p   p

8.   k   k   k

9.   m   m   m

10.   n   n   n

11.   l   l   l

12.   r   r   r

Dictation

1. le___on   2. ro___ot   3. pea___ut   4. ru___er

Write It

Letter Box

| b | f | r | k | m | p | d | l | n |

Say the word for the picture. Listen to the letter-sounds.
Write the missing letter.

1. 	2. 	3. 	4.
___ an	doo ___	ro ___ ot	___ at
5. 	6.	7.	8. 
coo ___	ru ___ er	___ uck	dru ___
9.	10.	11.	12.
pea ___ ut	___ en	toa ___	pa ___ er

Dictation

1. ___ og   2. ___ ip   3. ca ___ in   4. me ___ u   5. pa ___   6. ba ___

Initial, Medial, and Final Consonants
s, t, v, h, w, j, y, q, x, z

DAY 1 — **Listening for Initial and Final Consonants: s, t, v**

Read aloud the focus statement and point to each letter as you introduce its letter-sound. Say: *This is the letter s. The letter s is a consonant. It stands for this sound: /s/. Say /s/. (/s/) You hear /s/ at the beginning of surf. Say surf.* (surf) *You hear /s/ at the end of bus. Say bus.* (bus) Repeat the process for the letters **t** and **v**. Then read the directions and call students' attention to number 1. Say: *Say soap.* (soap) *Do you hear /s/ first or last in soap?* (first) *Fill in the first circle.* Repeat the process for the remaining pictures.

Picture Key: 1. soap, 2. salad, 3. gas, 4. tiger, 5. meat, 6. tape, 7. cave, 8. van, 9. vest

Dictation Direct students' attention to the bottom of the page and say:

(for numbers 1–3) *Write the letter that stands for the first sound you hear in _____.*   1. sit   2. tag   3. vet
(for numbers 4–6) *Write the letter that stands for the last sound you hear in _____.*   4. yes   5. nut   6. live

DAY 2 — **Listening for Initial Consonants: h, w, j, y**

Read aloud the focus statement. Then point to each letter as you introduce its letter-sound. Say: *This is the letter h. The letter h is a consonant. It stands for this sound: /h/. Say /h/. (/h/) You hear /h/ at the beginning of hand. Say hand.* (hand) Repeat the process for the letters **w**, **j**, and **y**. Point out that the letter **y** always has the /y/ sound when it appears at the beginning of a word. Then read the directions and call students' attention to number 1. Say: *The first picture shows a worm. What is the first sound in worm?* (/w/) *Which letter stands for that sound?* (w) *Circle the letter w.* Repeat the process for the remaining pictures.

Picture Key: 1. worm, 2. hook, 3. jeep, 4. yawn, 5. window, 6. jar, 7. heart, 8. horn, 9. yo-yo

Dictation Direct students' attention to the bottom of the page and say:

Write the letter that stands for the first sound you hear in _____.   1. hay   2. yes   3. wet   4. jazz   5. win   6. hip

DAY 3 — **Listening for Initial and Final Consonants: q, x, z**

Read aloud the focus statement. Then point to the letter **q** and say: *This is the letter q. It is always followed by the letter u. The letters q and u together have this sound: /kw/. Say /kw/. (/kw/) You hear /kw/ in queen. Say queen.* (queen) Then point to the letter **x** and say: *The letter x has this sound: /ks/. Say /ks/. (/ks/) You hear /ks/ at the end of fox. Say fox.* (fox) Repeat the process for **z**. Then read the directions and call students' attention to row 1. Say: *Say queen.* (queen) *Do you hear /kw/ in queen?* (yes) *Fill in the circle below the picture of the queen.* Repeat this process for the remaining pictures in each row.

Picture Key: Row 1: queen, quilt, vase, quarter; Row 2: box, yarn, fox, six; Row 3: zipper, zebra, ten, zoo

Dictation Direct students' attention to the bottom of the page and say:

(for numbers 1, 2) *Write the letter that stands for the first sound you hear in _____.*   1. quake   2. zebra
(for numbers 3–5) *Write the letter that stands for the last sound you hear in _____.*   3. quiz   4. wax   5. fix

DAY 4 — **Listening for Initial, Medial, and Final Consonants: t, v, j, x, z**

Read aloud the focus statement. Then point to the example as you say: *Say seven.* (seven) *What consonant sound do you hear in the middle?* (/v/) Then read aloud the directions and call students' attention to number 1. Say: *Point to the picture of a boat. What letters are below it?* (t) *What sound does t have?* (/t/) *Say boat.* (boat) *Do you hear /t/ first, last, or in the middle of boat?* (last) *Circle the last t.* Repeat the process for the remaining pictures.

Picture Key: 1. boat, 2. five, 3. jeep, 4. oxen, 5. puzzle, 6. beaver, 7. zebra, 8. tape, 9. meter, 10. fox, 11. net, 12. banjo

Dictation Direct students' attention to the bottom of the page and say:

Write the letter that stands for the middle sound you hear in _____.   1. exam   2. seven   3. meter

DAY 5 — **Writing Initial, Medial, and Final Consonants: s, t, v, h, w, j, y, q, x, z**

Read aloud the directions and call students' attention to number 1. Say: *Point to the zero. Say zero.* (zero) *What is the first sound in zero?* (/z/) *What letter stands for that sound?* (z) *Write the letter z on the line. You spelled the word zero.* Repeat the process for the remaining pictures.

Picture Key: 1. zero, 2. meter, 3. box, 4. soap, 5. quilt, 6. wig, 7. yawn, 8. shovel, 9. foot, 10. hook, 11. jump, 12. Texas

Dictation Direct students' attention to the bottom of the page and say:

Listen to this sentence: I put soap on my feet. Now write the missing letters.

Daily Phonics Practice • EMC 2790 • © Evan-Moor Corp.

Name _____

Listen for It

Focus The letters **s**, **t**, and **v** are consonants. Each consonant has a sound.

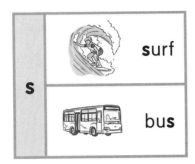 **s** — **s**urf / bu**s**

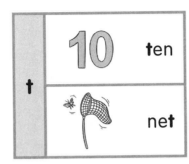 **t** — **t**en / ne**t**

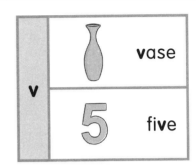 **v** — **v**ase / fi**v**e

Say the sound of the letter. Then say the word for the picture.
Fill in the circle to show if you hear the letter-sound **first** or **last**.

1.
s
◯——◯

2.
s
◯——◯

3.
s
◯——◯

4.
t
◯——◯

5.
t
◯——◯

6.
t
◯——◯

7.
v
◯——◯

8.
v
◯——◯

9.
v
◯——◯

Dictation •

1. ___it   2. ___ag   3. ___et   4. ye___   5. nu___   6. li___e

Listen for It

Focus | The letters **h**, **w**, **j**, and **y** are consonants. They have sounds that are usually heard at the **beginning** of a word.

h  **h**and	**w**  **w**eb	**j**  **j**et	**y**  **y**arn

Say the word for the picture.
Then circle the letter that stands for the **first** sound you hear.

1.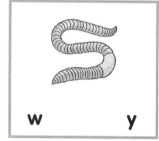
w   y

2.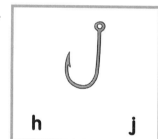
h   j

3.
h   j

4.
w   y

5.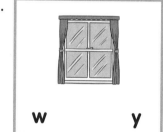
w   y

6.
h   j

7.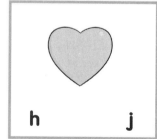
h   j

8.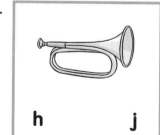
h   j

9.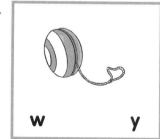
w   y

Dictation •

1. ___ay   2. ___es   3. ___et   4. ___azz   5. ___in   6. ___ip

Daily Phonics Practice • EMC 2790 • © Evan-Moor Corp.

Listen for It

Focus The letters **q**, **x**, and **z** are consonants. The letter **q** always appears with a **u** after it.

 **q** **q**ueen    **x** fo**x**    **z** **z**ero

Say the sound of the letter or letters. Then say the word for the picture.
Fill in the circle below the pictures that have the same sound.

1. **qu**
2. **x**
3. **z**

Dictation ....

1. ___uake   2. ___ebra   3. qui___   4. wa___   5. fi___

Name _____

Listen for It

Focus A word can begin or end with a consonant. A word can also have a consonant in the **middle**.

seven	7

Say the sound of the letter. Then say the word for the picture.
Circle the **first**, **middle**, or **last** letter to show where you hear the letter-sound.

1.
t   t   t

2.
v   v   v

3.
j   j   j

4.
x   x   x

5.
z   z   z

6.
v   v   v

7.
z   z   z

8.
t   t   t

9.
t   t   t

10.
x   x   x

11.
t   t   t

12.
j   j   j

Dictation ....

1. e___am   2. se___en   3. me___er

Skill: Discriminating initial, medial, and final consonants   Daily Phonics Practice • EMC 2790 • © Evan-Moor Corp.

Write It

Letter Box

| s | t | v | h | w | j | y | q | x | z |

Say the word for the picture. Listen to the letter-sounds.
Write the missing letter.

1. _____ero	2. me_____er	3. bo_____
4.  _____oap	5. _____uilt	6. _____ig
7. _____awn	8.  sho_____el	9. foo_____
10. _____ook	11. _____ump	12. Te_____as

Dictation

I pu_____ _____oap on my fee_____.

Skill: Writing initial, medial, and final consonants **15**

Short Vowel Sounds
a, e, i, o, u

DAY 1

Listening for Short Vowels: a, e

Read aloud the focus statement. Then point to the first example as you say: *Say the word* **bag.** (bag) *Say* /ă/. (/ă/) *That is the* **short a** *sound.* Repeat this process for the letter **e.** Then read the directions and call students' attention to number 1. Say: *Point to the can. Say* **can.** (can) *What vowel sound do you hear in* **can?** (/ă/) *What letter stands for that sound?* (a) *Fill in the circle next to the letter* **a.** Repeat the process for the remaining pictures.

Picture Key: 1. can, 2. bed, 3. rat, 4. belt, 5. hand, 6. jet, 7. sled, 8. elf, 9. flag

Dictation Direct students' attention to the bottom of the page and say:

Listen to each word I say. Then write the letter that stands for the short vowel sound you hear.
1. cab 2. net 3. best 4. hand 5. rat

DAY 2

Listening for Short Vowels: i, o, u

Read aloud the focus statement. Then point to the first example as you say: *Say the word* **mitt.** (mitt) *Say* /ĭ/. (/ĭ/) *That is the* **short i** *sound.* Repeat this process for the letters **o** and **u.** Then read the directions and call students' attention to number 1. Say: *Point to the sock. Say* **sock.** (sock) *What vowel sound do you hear in* **sock?** (/ŏ/) *What letter stands for that sound?* (o) *Fill in the circle next to the letter* **o.** Repeat the process for the remaining pictures.

Picture Key: 1. sock, 2. fish, 3. clock, 4. nuts, 5. tub, 6. fox, 7. gum, 8. dish, 9. chick

Dictation Direct students' attention to the bottom of the page and say:

Listen to each word I say. Then write the letter that stands for the short vowel sound you hear.
1. pup 2. wish 3. lid 4. mop 5. gum

DAY 3

Writing Short Vowels: a, e, i, o, u

Call students' attention to the letter box at the top of the page. Have students name each vowel and say its short sound aloud. Then read the directions and call students' attention to number 1. Say: *The picture shows a ham. Say* **ham.** (ham) *What short vowel sound do you hear in* **ham?** (/ă/) *What letter stands for /ă/?* (a) *Write the letter* **a** *on the line. Read the word with me:* **ham.** Repeat the process for the remaining pictures.

Picture Key: 1. ham, 2. cup, 3. mop, 4. lock, 5. leg, 6. bib, 7. back, 8. bed, 9. clam, 10. jump, 11. swim, 12. tent

Dictation Direct students' attention to the bottom of the page and say:

Listen to each word I say. Then write the letter that stands for the short vowel sound you hear.
1. bed 2. top 3. tin 4. run 5. sat

DAY 4

Reading Words with Short Vowel Sounds: a, e, i, o, u

Read aloud the directions and call students' attention to number 1. Say: *The picture shows a cat. Say* **cat.** (cat) *What short vowel sound do you hear in* **cat?** (/ă/) *Look at the words under the picture. Circle the word that says* **cat.** After students finish, ask: *How do you spell* **cat?** (c-a-t) Repeat the process for the remaining pictures.

Picture Key: 1. cat, 2. bug, 3. cut, 4. net, 5. pot, 6. hat, 7. hit, 8. nap, 9. hop

Dictation Direct students' attention to the bottom of the page and say:

Listen to each word I say. Then write the word.   *1. bug 2. big 3. bag 4. beg*

DAY 5

Reading Words with Short Vowel Sounds: a, e, i, o, u

Read the directions and call students' attention to number 1. Say: *The picture shows a man taking a nap. Let's read the incomplete sentence together:* **He _____ a _____.** *Now point to the words in the gray bar. Let's read them together:* **had, nip, nap.** *Which word belongs on the first line?* (had) *Write the word* **had** *on the first line. Which word belongs on the second line?* (nap) *Write the word* **nap** *on the second line.* After students have finished writing, say: *Now let's read the sentence together:* **He had a nap.** Repeat the process for the remaining sentences.

Dictation Direct students' attention to the bottom of the page and say:

Listen to this sentence: **I see a bug in the net.** *Now write the letters that stand for the sounds you hear in* **bug, net.** After students finish writing, read the sentence together.

Name _____

Listen for It

Focus The letters **a** and **e** are vowels. Vowels can have a **short** sound. You hear the **short** a sound, /ă/, in **bag**. You hear the **short e** sound, /ĕ/, in **web**.

| short **a** bag | | short **e** web | |

Say the word for the picture. Listen for the **short** vowel sound.
Fill in the circle next to the letter that stands for that sound.

1. ○ a ○ e

2.  ○ a ○ e

3. ○ a ○ e

4.  ○ a ○ e

5. ○ a ○ e

6.  ○ a ○ e

7.  ○ a ○ e

8.  ○ a ○ e

9.  ○ a ○ e

Dictation •

1. c___b   2. n___t   3. b___st   4. h___nd   5. r___t

Listen for It

Focus The letters **i**, **o**, and **u** are vowels. Vowels can have a **short** sound. You hear the **short i** sound, /ĭ/, in **mitt**. You hear the **short o** sound, /ŏ/, in **box**. You hear the **short u** sound, /ŭ/, in **cup**.

| short **i** mitt | | short **o** box | | short **u** cup | |

Say the word for the picture. Listen for the **short** vowel sound.
Fill in the circle next to the letter that stands for that sound.

1.
   ○ **i**
   ○ **o**

2.
   ○ **i**
   ○ **o**

3.
   ○ **i**
   ○ **o**

4.
   ○ **o**
   ○ **u**

5.
   ○ **o**
   ○ **u**

6.
   ○ **o**
   ○ **u**

7.
   ○ **i**
   ○ **u**

8.
   ○ **i**
   ○ **u**

9.
   ○ **i**
   ○ **u**

Dictation •

1. p__p   2. w__sh   3. l__d   4. m__p   5. g__m

Write It

Letter Box

| a | e | i | o | u |

Say the word for the picture.
Write the letter that stands for the **short** vowel sound you hear.

1.  h ___ m	2.  c ___ p	3.  m ___ p	4. l ___ ck
5.  l ___ g	6. b ___ b	7.  b ___ ck	8.  b ___ d
9. cl ___ m	10.  j ___ mp	11.  sw ___ m	12.  t ___ nt

Dictation ···

1. b ___ d   2. t ___ p   3. t ___ n   4. r ___ n   5. s ___ t

Skill: Identifying short vowel sounds   **19**

Read It

Say the word for the picture. Listen for the **short** vowel sound.
Circle the word that has the vowel sound you hear.

1.

cat   cot

2.

bag   bug

3.

cot   cut

4.

nut   net

5.

pot   pet

6.

hat   hot

7.

hut   hit

8.

nap   nip

9.

hip   hop

Dictation

1. _____   2. _____   3. _____   4. _____

     Daily Phonics Practice • EMC 2790 • © Evan-Moor Corp.

Read It

Write the two words that best complete the sentence.

1.

| had | nip | nap |

He _____ a _____.

2.

| bug | bed | big |

It is a _____ _____.

3.

| hop | Can | hip |

_____ he _____?

4.

| cot | cat | sat |

The _____ _____ on it.

Dictation

I see a _____ in the _____.

DAY 1 **Listening for Medial Vowels**

Read aloud the focus statement. Then point to the word **van** and run your finger under each letter as you say: *This word is spelled with the consonant **v**, the vowel **a**, and the consonant **n**. The **a** in the middle has a short sound. Say **van**.* (van) Repeat the process for the remaining example words. Then read the directions and call students' attention to number 1. Say: *The picture shows a web. Say **web**.* (web) *What vowel sound do you hear in **web**?* (/ĕ/) *What letter stands for that sound?* (e) *Write the letter **e** on the line to spell the word **web**.* After students finish writing, read the word together. Repeat this process for the remaining CVC words.

Picture Key: 1. web, 2. pin, 3. rat, 4. bus, 5. fin, 6. gas, 7. ten, 8. box, 9. cub

Dictation Direct students' attention to the bottom of the page and say:

Listen to each word I say. Then write the word. 1. sad 2. sit 3. hug 4. box

DAY 2 **Reading CVC Words**

Read aloud the focus statement. Then read aloud the directions and call students' attention to number 1. Say: *This is a pot. Say **pot**.* (pot) *Look at the words next to the picture. Fill in the circle next to the word that says **pot**.* After students finish, ask: *How do you spell **pot**?* (p-o-t) Repeat the process for the remaining pictures.

Picture Key: 1. pot, 2. rip, 3. bat, 4. cob, 5. wig, 6. nuts, 7. hut, 8. bed, 9. pen

Dictation Direct students' attention to the bottom of the page and say:

Listen to each word I say. Then write the word. 1. not 2. net 3. nut 4. tip 5. tap

DAY 3 **Writing CVC Words**

Call students' attention to the word box at the top of the page. Guide students in reading each word aloud. Then read the directions and call students' attention to number 1. Say: *The picture shows a fox. Say **fox**.* (fox) *Find the word **fox** in the word box and write it on the line below the picture.* After students finish writing, ask: *How do you spell **fox**?* (f-o-x) Repeat this process for the remaining pictures.

Picture Key: 1. fox, 2. men, 3. cap, 4. fan, 5. tub, 6. cut, 7. pig, 8. leg, 9. mop

Dictation Direct students' attention to the bottom of the page and say:

Listen to each word I say. Then write the word. 1. lip 2. red 3. top 4. gum 5. man

DAY 4 **Writing CVC Words**

Read the directions and call students' attention to number 1. Say: *The picture shows a piece of paper being cut. Say **cut**.* (cut) *Now look at the word next to the picture. It is missing a vowel. Circle the vowel you hear in **cut** and write the word **cut** on the line.* Repeat the process for the remaining words.

Picture Key: 1. cut, 2. jet, 3. cot, 4. van, 5. mix

Dictation Direct students' attention to the bottom of the page and say:

*Listen to this sentence: **The bed is in the hut**. Now write the missing words: **bed, hut**.* After students finish writing, read the sentence together.

DAY 5 **Reading CVC Words**

Read the directions and call students' attention to number 1. Say: *The picture shows a bus. Let's read the incomplete sentence together: **Go get a _____ for the _____**. Now point to the words in the gray bar. Let's read them together: **bus, map, bug**. Which word belongs on the first line?* (map) *Write the word **map** on the first line. Which word belongs on the second line?* (bus) *Write the word **bus** on the second line.* After students have finished writing, say: *Now let's read the sentence together: **Go get a map for the bus**.* Repeat the process for the remaining sentences.

Dictation Direct students' attention to the bottom of the page and say:

*Listen to this sentence: **Do you see a bus or a cab?** Now write the missing words: **bus, cab**.* After students finish writing, read the sentence together.

Listen for It

Focus Words that have a vowel between two consonants are called consonant-vowel-consonant words, or **CVC words**. The vowel in a CVC word has a **short** sound.

va n

bed

pig

mop

nuts

Say the word for the picture. Listen for the **short** vowel sound.
Write the letter that stands for that sound.

1. w ___ b	2. p ___ n	3.  r ___ t
4.  b ___ s	5.  f ___ n	6. g ___ s
7. t ___ n	8. b ___ x	9. c ___ b

Dictation •••

1. _____   2. _____   3. _____   4. _____

Name _____

Read It

Focus A vowel between two consonants has a **short** sound.

Say the word for the picture. Listen to the **short** vowel sound.
Fill in the circle next to the word that has that vowel sound.

1.

○ pit
○ pot

2.

○ rip
○ rap

3.

○ bat
○ bet

4.

○ cab
○ cob

5.

○ wig
○ wag

6.

○ not
○ nuts

7.

○ hut
○ hat

8.

○ bud
○ bed

9.

○ pen
○ pan

Dictation ••

1. _____ 2. _____ 3. _____ 4. _____ 5. _____

Name _____

Write It

Word Box

tub	fox	fan
cut	mop	pig
men	leg	cap

Write the word that names the picture.

1.

_____

2.

_____

3.

_____

4.

_____

5.

_____

6.

_____

7.

_____

8.

_____

9.

_____

Dictation

1. _____ 2. _____ 3. _____ 4. _____ 5. _____

Write It

Say the word for the picture. Circle the letter that stands for
the **short** vowel sound you hear. Then write the word on the line.

1.   c _ t   a e i o u   _____

2.    j _ t   a e i o u   _____

3.    c _ t   a e i o u   _____

4.    v _ n   a e i o u   _____

5.    m _ x   a e i o u   _____

Dictation •••

The _____ is in the _____.

Read It

Write the two words that best complete the sentence.

1.

bus   map   bug

Go get a _____ for the _____.

2.

lot   sit   let

Will you _____ me _____ by you?

3.

van   red   rib

The _____ is _____.

4.

cab   nut   not

I did _____ go in a _____.

Dictation

Do you see a _____ or a _____?

Long Vowel Sounds
a, e, i, o, u

DAY 1

Listening for Long Vowels: a, e

Read aloud the focus statement. Then point to the first example as you say: *The long sound of a is /ā/. Say /ā/. (/ā/) Say tape.* (tape) Repeat the process for the letter **e**. Then read the directions and call students' attention to number 1. Say: *The picture shows two feet. Say feet.* (feet) *What long vowel sound do you hear in feet?* (/ē/) *What letter stands for that sound?* (e) *Circle the e.* Repeat the process for the remaining pictures.

Picture Key: 1. feet, 2. safe, 3. rake, 4. read, 5. cake, 6. snail, 7. seal, 8. sheep, 9. game

Dictation Direct students' attention to the bottom of the page and say:

Listen to each word I say. Then write the letter that stands for the long vowel sound you hear.
1. ape   2. we   3. he   4. same

DAY 2

Listening for Long Vowels: i, o, u

Read aloud the focus statement. Then point to the first example as you say: *The long sound of i is /ī/. Say /ī/. (/ī/) Say kite.* (kite) Repeat the process for the letters **o** and **u**. Then read the directions and call students' attention to number 1. Say: *The picture shows a toad. Say toad.* (toad) *What long vowel sound do you hear in toad?* (/ō/) *What letter stands for that sound?* (o) *Circle the o.* Repeat the process for the remaining pictures.

Picture Key: 1. toad, 2. dime, 3. soap, 4. tire, 5. cube, 6. bone, 7. tube, 8. goat, 9. nine

Dictation Direct students' attention to the bottom of the page and say:

Listen to each word I say. Then write the letter that stands for the long vowel sound you hear.
1. mule   2. home   3. bite   4. code

DAY 3

Writing Long Vowels: a, e, i, o, u

Call students' attention to the letter box at the top of the page. Have them point to each vowel and say its long sound aloud. Then read the directions and call students' attention to number 1. Say: *This shows a person who dives underwater. Say dive.* (dive) *What long vowel sound do you hear in dive?* (/ī/) *What letter stands for that sound?* (i) *Write the letter i on the line. You spelled the word dive. Now let's read the word together: dive.* Then explain: *Many words with a long vowel sound have a silent e at the end. The e at the end of dive is silent.* Repeat the process for the remaining words.

Picture Key: 1. dive, 2. vase, 3. bone, 4. nose, 5. mice, 6. tube, 7. me, 8. cube, 9. rake

Dictation Direct students' attention to the bottom of the page and say:

Listen to each word I say. Then write the letter that stands for the long vowel sound you hear.
1. we   2. like   3. cake   4. rope   5. rule

DAY 4

Writing Long Vowels: a, e, i, o, u

Read the directions and call students' attention to number 1. Say: *The picture shows a lake. Say lake.* (lake) *What long vowel sound do you hear in lake?* (/ā/) *What letter stands for that sound?* (a) *Write the letter a on the line. You spelled the word lake. Now let's read the word together: lake. Remember, the e at the end of lake is silent.* Repeat the process for the remaining words.

Picture Key: 1. lake, 2. me, 3. kite, 4. rope, 5. mule, 6. we, 7. hose, 8. tape, 9. bike

Dictation Direct students' attention to the bottom of the page and say:

Listen to each word I say. Then write the letter that stands for the long vowel sound you hear.
1. be   2. time   3. nose   4. tube   5. he

DAY 5

Reading Words with Long Vowel Sounds: a, e, i, o, u

Read the directions and call students' attention to the picture. Say: *This picture shows two guys making a cake. Let's read the first incomplete sentence together: We will _____ a _____. Now let's read the words in the gray bar together: rake, cake, bake. Which word belongs on the first line?* (bake) *Write bake on the first line. Which word belongs on the second line?* (cake) *Write the word cake on the second line.* After students finish writing, say: *Now let's read the sentence together: We will bake a cake.* Repeat the process for the remaining sentences.

Dictation Direct students' attention to the bottom of the page and say:

Listen to this sentence: We like your cape. Now write the letters that stand for the long vowel sounds you hear in We, like, and cape. After students finish writing, read the sentence together.

Daily Phonics Practice • EMC 2790 • © Evan-Moor Corp.

Listen for It

A vowel can have a **long** sound. The long sound says the vowel's name. You hear the **long a** sound in **tape**. You hear the **long e** sound in **me**.

| long **a** tape | long **e** me |

Say the word for the picture. Listen to the **long** vowel sound.
Circle the letter that stands for that sound.

1.

a   e

2.

a   e

3.

a   e

4.

a   e

5.

a   e

6.

a   e

7.

a   e

8.

a   e

9.

a   e

Dictation •••

1. ___pe   2. w___   3. h___   4. s___me

Listen for It

Focus A vowel can have a **long** sound. The long sound says the vowel's name. You hear the **long i** sound in **kite**. You hear the **long o** sound in **hose**. You hear the **long u** sound in **mule**.

| long **i** kite | long **o** hose | long **u** mule |

Say the word for the picture. Listen to the **long** vowel sound.
Circle the letter that stands for that sound.

1. i   o   u

2. i   o   u

3. i   o   u

4. i   o   u

5. i   o   u

6. i   o   u

7. i   o   u

8. i   o   u

9. i   o   u

Dictation •

1. m___le   2. h___me   3. b___te   4. c___de

Name _____

Write It

Letter Box

a   e   i   o   u

Say the word for the picture.
Write the letter that stands for the **long** vowel sound you hear.

1.  d ___ ve	2.  v ___ se	3.  b ___ ne
4. n ___ se	5.  m ___ ce	6. t ___ be
7.  m ___	8. c ___ be	9.  r ___ ke

Dictation

1. W___   2. l___ke   3. c___ke   4. r___pe   5. r___le

Write It

Letter Box

a   e   i   o   u

Say the word for the picture.
Write the letter that stands for the **long** vowel sound you hear.

1.  l ___ ke	2.  m ___	3.  k ___ te
4. r ___ pe	5.  m ___ le	6.  w ___
7. h ___ se	8. t ___ pe	9.  b ___ ke

Dictation

1. b___   2. t___me   3. n___se   4. t___be   5. h___

Read It

Write the two words that best complete the sentence.

| rake   cake   bake |

1. We will _____ a _____ .

| Pete   be   me |

2. _____ will help _____ .

| rose   hope   bone |

3. I _____ to make a _____ .

| tube   cute   use |

4. We can _____ this _____ .

| time   fine   kite |

5. The cake looks _____ this _____ .

Dictation

W___ l___ke your c___pe.

Skill: Reading words with long vowel sounds   **33**

CVCe Words

DAY 1 — Reading CVCe Words

Read aloud the focus statement. Then point to the example as you explain the CVCe pattern. Say: *This word says **can**. It is a CVC word. It has a **short a** sound in the middle. When we add a silent **e** to **can**, it becomes the word **cane**. Now it is a **CVCe** word. The final **e** is silent but it makes the letter **a** have the **long a** sound. Say **can**.* (can) *Say **cane**.* (cane) Then read the directions and call students' attention to number 1. Say: *We are going to add a final **e** to CVC words to make the vowel sound in the middle **long**. Let's read the first word: **man**. Write an **e** on the line to make the vowel sound in the middle long. Now read the new word: **mane**. Which of these pictures shows a lion's **mane**?* (the second one) *Fill in the circle below the picture that shows a mane.* Repeat the process for the remaining words.

Picture Key: 1. man, mane; 2. cut, cute; 3. pin, pine; 4. rod, rode; 5. rob, robe; 6. tub, tube

Dictation Direct students' attention to the bottom of the page and say:

Listen to each word I say. Then write the missing letter or letters. 1. *cub* 2. *cube* 3. *rat* 4. *rate*

DAY 2 — Writing Long Vowels in CVCe Words

Read the directions and call students' attention to number 1. Say: *The picture shows a robe. Say **robe**.* (robe) *What long vowel sound do you hear in **robe**?* (long o; /ō/) *Write the letter **o** on the first line. Now write a silent **e** at the end of the word to make the **o** have a **long** vowel sound. Let's read the word together: **robe**.* Repeat the process for the remaining pictures.

Picture Key: 1. robe, 2. hive, 3. cube, 4. cake, 5. cane, 6. bike, 7. rose, 8. kite, 9. tape

Dictation Direct students' attention to the bottom of the page and say:

Listen to each word I say. Then write the word that you hear. 1. *robe* 2. *tube* 3. *cake* 4. *like*

DAY 3 — Writing CVCe Words

Call students' attention to the word box at the top of the page. Have students read each word aloud. Then read the directions and call students' attention to number 1. Say: *This is a rope. Say **rope**.* (rope) *Find the word **rope** in the word box. How is **rope** spelled?* (r-o-p-e) *Write the word **rope** on the line.* Repeat the process for the remaining pictures.

Picture Key: 1. rope, 2. cake, 3. bike, 4. mule, 5. vase, 6. kite, 7. tube, 8. robe

Dictation Direct students' attention to the bottom of the page and say:

Listen to each word I say. Then write the word that you hear. 1. *pine* 2. *same* 3. *poke* 4. *rule*

DAY 4 — Reading CVCe Words

Read the directions and call students' attention to number 1. Say: *The first picture shows a clock. A clock tells us what time it is. Say **time**.* (time) *What long vowel sound do you hear in **time**?* (long i; /ī/) *Read the words in the row. Which one says **time**?* (the second one) *How do you spell **time**?* (t-i-m-e) *Circle the word **time**.* Repeat the process for the remaining rows. For the word **pane** in row 2, you may need to explain that this word is spelled differently than the word **pain**, which means "something that hurts."

Dictation Direct students' attention to the bottom of the page and say:

Listen to each word I say. Then write the word that you hear. 1. *hive* 2. *save* 3. *hike* 4. *code*

DAY 5 — Reading CVCe Words

Read aloud the directions and call students' attention to the picture. Say: *This picture shows kids next to a lake. Let's read the first incomplete sentence together: **You can** _____ **a** _____. Now let's read the words in the gray bar together: **mule, ride, mole**. Which word belongs on the first line?* (ride) *Write **ride** on the first line. Now you know which word to write on the next line.* After students finish writing, say: *Now let's read the sentence together: **You can ride a mule**.* Repeat the process for the remaining sentences.

Dictation Direct students' attention to the bottom of the page and say:

*Listen to this sentence: **I hope we have a cake**. Now write the sentence on the line.*

Read It

Focus Some words have a **CVCe** pattern. The vowel in the middle has a **long** sound. The **e** at the end is silent.

| | can + **e** = cane | |

Read the word. Write a final **e** to make a new word.
Then fill in the circle under the picture that matches the new word.

1.

man___

○   ○

2.

cut___

○   ○

3.

pin___

○   ○

4.

rod___

○   ○

5.

rob___

○   ○

6.

tub___

○   ○

Dictation •

1. c___b   2. c___b___   3. r___t   4. r___t___

Write It

Letter Box

a   e   i   o   u

Say the word for the picture. Write the letter that stands for the **long** vowel sound.
Then write the silent **e** at the end and read the word.

1.  r ___ b ___	2.  h ___ v ___	3. c ___ b ___
4.  c ___ k ___	5.  c ___ n ___	6.  b ___ k ___
7.  r ___ s ___	8.  k ___ t ___	9. t ___ p ___

Dictation

1. _____   2. _____   3. _____   4. _____

Write It

Word Box

pine	cake	bike	rope	vase
kite	tube	robe	mule	dine

Write the word that names the picture.

1.
_____

2.
_____

3.
_____

4.
_____

5.
_____

6.
_____

7.
_____

8.
_____

Dictation

1. _____ 2. _____ 3. _____ 4. _____

Read It

Look at the picture. Read the words.
Circle the word that names the picture.

1.		tame	time
2.		pane	pine
3.		mile	mule
4.		cake	cape
5.		fire	fine
6.		like	lake
7.		tire	tore

Dictation

1. _____   2. _____   3. _____   4. _____

Read It

Write the two words that best complete the sentence.

> mule   ride   mole

1. You can _____ a _____.

> like   hike   lake

2. Pete and I can _____ to the _____.

> hole   hope   cute

3. There is a _____ fox in the _____.

> pine   dine   tube

4. You can _____ under a _____.

> tide   time   take

5. We can _____ our _____.

Dictation •

_____

Long Vowel Sounds of y

DAY 1

Listening for the Long e and Long i Sounds of y

Read aloud the focus statement. Then point to the first example as you say: *The word* **jelly** *ends with a* **y** *after the consonant* **l**. *Say* **jelly**. (jelly) *You hear the* **long e** *at the end of* **jelly**. Then point to the word **cry** and say: *The word* **cry** *ends with a* **y** *after the consonant* **r**. *Say* **cry**. (cry) *You can hear the* **long i** *sound at the end of* **cry**. Then read the directions and call students' attention to number 1. Say: *The picture shows an egg frying in a pan. Say* **fry**. (fry) *Now read the word with me:* **fry**. *What sound does the* **y** *in* **fry** *have?* (long i; /ī/) *Draw a line from the picture to the box that says* **long i**. Repeat the process for the remaining words.

Dictation   Direct students' attention to the bottom of the page and say:

Listen to each word I say. Then write the word that you hear. Each word ends with the letter **y**.
1. *sky*   2. *pony*   3. *candy*   4. *cry*

DAY 2

Listening for the Long e and Long i Sounds of y

Read aloud the focus statement. Then point to the first example and say: *Say* **cry**. (cry) *How many vowel sounds do you hear in* **cry**? (1) *Yes,* **cry** *has one vowel sound:* /ī/. *So how many syllables does* **cry** *have?* (1) *Right, words that have one vowel sound have one syllable.* Repeat the process for **baby**. Then read the directions and call students' attention to number 1. Say: *The picture shows a penny. Say* **penny**. (penny) *How many vowel sounds do you hear in* **penny**? (2) *So how many syllables does* **penny** *have?* (2) *Fill in the circle next to the number 2. What sound does the* **y** *in* **penny** *have?* (/ē/, long e) *Fill in the circle next to the letter* **e**. Repeat the process for the remaining words.

Dictation   Direct students' attention to the bottom of the page and say:

Listen to each word I say. Then write the word that you hear. Each word ends with the letter **y**.
1. *penny*   2. *lady*   3. *fry*   4. *fly*

DAY 3

Writing Words with the Long Vowel Sounds of y

Read aloud the directions and call students' attention to the word box. Have them read each word aloud. Then say: *Point to the first word. What does it say?* (rusty) *Does the letter* **y** *have the* **long e** *or the* **long i** *sound in* **rusty**? (long e) *Write the word* **rusty** *on the line in the box that says* **y = long e**. Repeat the process for the remaining words.

Dictation   Direct students' attention to the bottom of the page and say:

Listen to this sentence: **She is a sly lady.** *Write the missing words on the lines.*

DAY 4

Reading Words with the Long Vowel Sounds of y

Read aloud the directions and call students' attention to number 1. Say: *The picture shows a baby. Read each word in the row. Which word says* **baby**? (the second one) *How do you spell* **baby**? (b-a-b-y) *Circle the word* **baby**. Repeat the process for the remaining rows.

Dictation   Direct students' attention to the bottom of the page and say:

Listen to this sentence. Then write it on the line: **A spy is not lazy.**

DAY 5

Reading Words with the Long Vowel Sounds of y

Read aloud the directions and call students' attention to the picture. Say: *This picture shows ponies in a stable. Let's read the first incomplete sentence together:* **I like to ride** _____ _____. *Now let's read the words in the gray bar together:* **me, pony, my**. *Which word belongs on the first line?* (my) *Write* **my** *on the first line. Now you know which word to write on the next line.* After students finish writing, say: *Now let's read the sentence together:* **I like to ride my pony.** Repeat the process for the remaining sentences.

Dictation   Direct students' attention to the bottom of the page and say:

Listen to this sentence. Then write it on the line: **It is sunny and windy.**

Listen for It

Focus — Many words end with the letter **y**. When the **y** comes after a consonant, the **y** can have a **long e** or a **long i** sound.

| **y** = long **e** jell**y** | | **y** = long **i** cr**y** |  |

Say the word for the picture. Do you hear **long e** or **long i**?
Draw a line from the word to **long e** or **long i**.

1.
fry

2.
windy

3.
pony

4.
baby

long
e

long
i

5.
fly

6.
candy

7.
sky

8.
mummy

Dictation

1. _____   2. _____   3. _____   4. _____

Listen for It

Focus A **syllable** is a word part that has one vowel sound. A **y** usually has the **long i** sound at the end of a word that has one syllable. A **y** usually has the **long e** sound at the end of a word that has two syllables.

y = long **i** cry		**1** syllable

y = long **e** baby		**2** syllables

Say the word. How many syllables do you hear?
Fill in the circle next to that number.
Then fill in the circle next to **i** or **e** to show what sound the **y** has.

1. penny

syllables	y
○ 1	○ i
○ 2	○ e

2. sunny

syllables	y
○ 1	○ i
○ 2	○ e

3. sky

syllables	y
○ 1	○ i
○ 2	○ e

4. lady

syllables	y
○ 1	○ i
○ 2	○ e

5. fry

syllables	y
○ 1	○ i
○ 2	○ e

6.  fly

syllables	y
○ 1	○ i
○ 2	○ e

Dictation

1. _____ 2. _____ 3. _____ 4. _____

Write It

Word Box

rusty	mummy	dry	penny	spy
cry	my	windy	sly	lazy

Read each word. Do you hear **long e** or **long i**?
Write the word in the correct box.

y = long e	**y = long i**
_____	_____
_____	_____
_____	_____
_____	_____
_____	_____

Dictation •

She is a _____ _____.

Read It

Look at the picture. Read the words. Circle the word that names the picture.

#			
1.	 lazy	baby	lady
2.	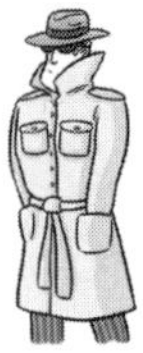 dry	spy	cry
3.	 windy	try	foggy
4.	 penny	sly	fry
5.	 candy	sandy	silly
6.	 muddy	mummy	my
7.	 fly	rusty	jelly

Dictation ••

_____

_____

Read It

Write the two words that best complete the sentence.

| me | pony | my |

1. I like to ride _____ _____.

| sky | sandy | sunny |

2. We ride when the _____ is _____.

| cry | dusty | dry |

3. My face gets _____ and _____.

| muddy | funny | try |

4. At the lake, I _____ not to get _____.

| happy | lazy | windy |

5. I am _____ that my pony is not _____.

Dictation

_____

Hard and Soft c and g

DAY 1 — Listening for Hard and Soft c

Read aloud the focus statement. Then point to the first example and say: *Say the words **cat**, **cot**, and **cup**.* (cat, cot, cup) *What sound do you hear at the beginning of **cat**, **cot**, and **cup**?* (/k/) *That is the **hard c** sound.* Repeat the process for **face** and **city**. Then read aloud the directions and call students' attention to number 1. Say: *The picture shows an ice-cream cone. Say **cone**.* (cone) *Now look at the word **cone**. What letter comes after the c?* (o) *What sound does the c have in **cone**?* (/k/) *Is that the sound of **hard c** or **soft c**?* (hard c) *Fill in the circle below **hard c**.* Repeat the process for the remaining words.

Dictation   Direct students' attention to the bottom of the page and say:

Listen to each word I say. Then write the word you hear.   1. cat   2. city   3. cut   4. mice

DAY 2 — Writing Words with Hard and Soft c

Direct students' attention to the word box at the top of the page. Guide them in reading each word aloud. Then read aloud the directions and call students' attention to the first word in the word box. Ask: *What does this word say?* (mice) *Do you hear /k/ or /s/ in **mice**?* (/s/) *Write **mice** in the box that says **soft c**, /s/.* Repeat the process for the remaining words.

Dictation   Direct students' attention to the bottom of the page and say:

Listen to each word I say. Then write the word you hear.   1. cub   2. nice   3. pencil   4. cone

DAY 3 — Listening for Hard and Soft g

Read aloud the focus statement. Then point to the first example and say: *Say the words **game**, **golf**, and **gull**.* (game, golf, gull) *What sound do you hear at the beginning of **game**, **golf**, and **gull**?* (/g/) *That is the **hard g** sound.* Repeat the process for **gem** and **giraffe**. Then read aloud the directions and call students' attention to number 1. Say: *The picture shows a giant. Say **giant**.* (giant) *Now look at the word **giant**. What sound does the g have in **giant**?* (/j/) *Is that the sound of **hard g** or **soft g**?* (soft g) *Fill in the circle below **soft g**.* Repeat the process for the remaining words.

Dictation   Direct students' attention to the bottom of the page and say:

Listen to each word I say. Then write the word you hear.   1. game   2. gem   3. gum   4. grant

DAY 4 — Writing Words with Hard and Soft g

Direct students' attention to the word box at the top of the page. Guide them in reading each word aloud. Then read aloud the directions and call students' attention to the first word in the word box. Ask: *What does this word say?* (page) *Do you hear /g/ or /j/ in **page**?* (/j/) *Write **page** in the box that says **soft g**, /j/.* Repeat the process for the remaining words.

Dictation   Direct students' attention to the bottom of the page and say:

Listen to each word I say. Then write the word you hear.   1. wage   2. gap   3. cage   4. golf

DAY 5 — Reading Words with Hard and Soft c and g

Read aloud the directions and call students' attention to the picture. Say: *This picture shows mice eating rice.* Say: *Let's read the first incomplete sentence together: **I had a _____ bag of _____.** Now let's read the words in the gray bar together: **gem**, **rice**, **giant**. Which word belongs on the first line?* (giant) *Write **giant** on the first line. Which word belongs on the second line?* (rice) *Write **rice** on the second line. Now let's read the sentence together: **I had a giant bag of rice.*** Have students complete the remaining sentences independently. Then read the completed sentences together.

Dictation   Direct students' attention to the bottom of the page and say:

*Listen to this sentence. Then write it on the line: **The fence has a gate.***

Name _____

Listen for It

Focus The letter **c** can have the **hard** sound of **/k/** or the **soft** sound of **/s/**. The **c** has the **/k/** sound when it is followed by an **a**, an **o**, or a **u**. The **c** has the **/s/** sound when it is followed by an **e** or an **i**.

c = /k/ sound		
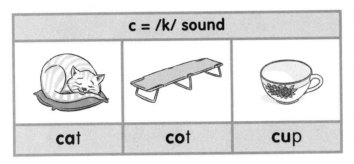		
cat	**co**t	**cu**p

c = /s/ sound	
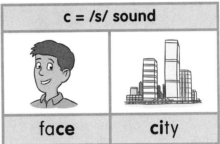	
fa**ce**	**ci**ty

Say the word and listen for the sound of **c**.
Fill in the circle below **hard c** or **soft c**.

1. cone

hard c   soft c
○   ○

2. mice

hard c   soft c
○   ○

3. pencil

hard c   soft c
○   ○

4. cart

hard c   soft c
○   ○

5. rice

hard c   soft c
○   ○

6. vacuum
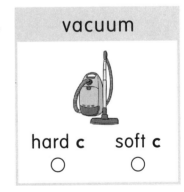
hard c   soft c
○   ○

Dictation

1. _____   2. _____   3. _____   4. _____

Write It

Word Box

mice	cone	city	cube
cake	rice	cast	fence
cuff	cod	cent	pencil

Read each word. Listen for the sound of **hard c** or **soft c**.
Write the word in the correct box.

hard **c** /k/	soft **c** /s/
_____	_____
_____	_____
_____	_____
_____	_____
_____	_____
_____	_____

Dictation

1. _____   2. _____   3. _____   4. _____

Listen for It

The letter **g** usually has the **hard** sound of /g/ when the next letter is **a**, **o**, or **u**. The letter **g** usually has the **soft** sound of /j/ when the next letter is **e** or **i**.

g = /g/ sound			g = /j/ sound	
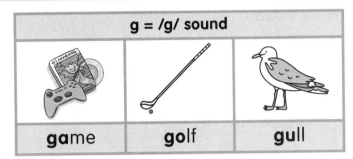			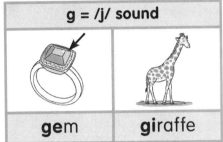	
game	**go**lf	**gu**ll	**ge**m	**gi**raffe

Say the word and listen for the sound of **g**.
Fill in the circle below **hard g** or **soft g**.

1. giant

hard **g**   soft **g**
○   ○

2. gum

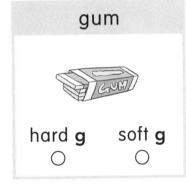

hard **g**   soft **g**
○   ○

3. huge

hard **g**   soft **g**
○   ○

4. gas

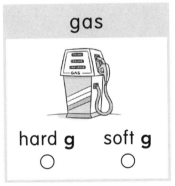

hard **g**   soft **g**
○   ○

5. wagon

hard **g**   soft **g**
○   ○

6. gate

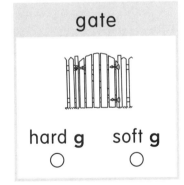

hard **g**   soft **g**
○   ○

Dictation ··

1. _____   2. _____   3. _____   4. _____

Write It

Word Box

page	gem	game	orange
huge	gum	wage	wagon
gate	gust	golf	giant

Read each word. Listen for the sound of **hard g** or **soft g**.
Write the word in the correct box.

hard **g** /g/	soft **g** /j/
_____	_____
_____	_____
_____	_____
_____	_____
_____	_____
_____	_____

Dictation

1. _____ 2. _____ 3. _____ 4. _____

Name _____

Read It

Write the two words that best complete the sentence.

| gem | rice | giant |

1. I had a _____ bag of _____.

| cat | hug | huge |

2. My _____ made a _____ hole in the bag.

| cute | mice | cut |

3. Two _____ _____ ate the rice.

| got | orange | gate |

4. An _____ bug also _____ into the rice.

| gave | cave | nice |

5. I _____ the rest of the rice to a _____ dog.

Dictation

....

_____

_____

Initial Consonant Blends
with s, r, or l

DAY 1 **Listening for Initial Consonant Blends: sk, sm, sn, sp, st, sw**
Read aloud the focus statement. Then point to the first example and say: *The letters **s** and **k** blend together to make this sound: /**sk**/. Say /**sk**/. (/sk/) You hear /**sk**/ in the word **sky**. Say **sky**.* (sky) Repeat this process for the remaining examples. Then read aloud the directions and call students' attention to number 1. Say: *Say **spoon**.* (spoon) *What blend do you hear at the beginning of **spoon**?* (/sp/) *What letters stand for that sound?* (sp) *Fill in the circle next to the letters **sp**.* Repeat this process for the remaining pictures.
Picture Key: 1. spoon, 2. space, 3. smoke, 4. swan, 5. stamp, 6. snail, 7. skunk, 8. swing, 9. spider

Dictation Direct students' attention to the bottom of the page and say:
Listen to each word I say. Then write the letters that stand for the blend you hear. 1. smile 2. snip 3. stand 4. spot

DAY 2 **Listening for Initial Consonant Blends: br, cr, dr, fr, gr, pr, tr**
Read aloud the focus statement. Then point to the first example and say: *The letters **b** and **r** blend together to make this sound: /**br**/. Say /**br**/. (/br/) You hear /**br**/ in the word **bran**. Say **bran**.* (bran) Repeat this process for the remaining examples. Then read aloud the directions and call students' attention to number 1. Say: *Say **truck**.* (truck) *What blend do you hear at the beginning of **truck**?* (/tr/) *What letters stand for that sound?* (tr) *Fill in the circle next to the letters **tr**.* Repeat this process for the remaining pictures.
Picture Key: 1. truck, 2. grapes, 3. drum, 4. crab, 5. bride, 6. crown, 7. frog, 8. prize, 9. grill

Dictation Direct students' attention to the bottom of the page and say:
Listen to each word I say. Then write the letters that stand for the blend you hear. 1. crab 2. trap 3. pride 4. grin

DAY 3 **Listening for Initial Consonant Blends: bl, cl, fl, gl, pl, sl**
Read aloud the focus statement. Then point to the first example and say: *The letters **b** and **l** blend together to make this sound: /**bl**/. Say /**bl**/. (/bl/) You hear /**bl**/ in the word **block**. Say **block**.* (block) Repeat this process for the remaining examples. Then read aloud the directions and call students' attention to number 1. Say: *Say **flag**.* (flag) *What blend do you hear at the beginning of **flag**?* (/fl/) *What letters stand for that sound?* (fl) *Fill in the circle next to the letters **fl**.* Repeat this process for the remaining pictures.
Picture Key: 1. flag, 2. clothes, 3. slippers, 4. glue, 5. blanket, 6. pliers, 7. glove, 8. plug, 9. flute

Dictation Direct students' attention to the bottom of the page and say:
Listen to each word I say. Then write the letters that stand for the blend you hear. 1. blog 2. slim 3. plan 4. clip

DAY 4 **Writing Initial Consonant Blends: bl, cr, dr, fl, gl, gr, sp, st**
Direct students' attention to the letter box at the top of the page. Guide students in saying each blend aloud. Then read aloud the directions and call students' attention to number 1. Say: *Say **glove**.* (glove) *What blend do you hear in **glove**?* (/gl/) *What letters stand for that sound?* (gl) *Write the letters **gl** on the lines. You spelled the word **glove**. Let's read it together: **glove**.* Repeat this process for the remaining pictures.
Picture Key: 1. glove, 2. stamp, 3. drum, 4. stop, 5. crab, 6. flag, 7. grill, 8. space, 9. block, 10. glue, 11. flower, 12. draw

Dictation Direct students' attention to the bottom of the page and say:
Listen to each word I say. Then write the word on the line. 1. flip 2. slip 3. drip 4. snip

DAY 5 **Reading Words with Initial Consonant Blends: sl, st, sw, cr, dr, fr, gr, tr, fl, gl**
Direct students' attention to the picture. Say: *This picture shows someone swimming in a pool. Let's read the first incomplete sentence together: **I can _____ like a _____.** Now let's read the words in the gray bar: **slim, frog, swim**. Which word belongs on the first line?* (swim) *Write **swim** on the first line. Which word will make sense on the second line?* (frog) *Write **frog** on the second line.* (pause) *Now let's read the sentence together: **I can swim like a frog**.* Repeat this process for the remaining sentences.

Dictation Direct students' attention to the bottom of the page and say:
*Listen to this sentence. Then write it on the line: **I am in the swim club**.* (pause) *Circle each blend in the sentence.*

Listen for It

Focus Two consonant sounds said together are called a **consonant blend.** Many words begin with a blend that starts with **s.**

sk	sm	sn	sp	st	sw
sky	**sm**ile	**sn**ap	**sp**ell	**st**ar	**sw**eep

Say the word for the picture.
Fill in the circle next to the blend you hear at the beginning of the word.

1.
○ sk
○ sm
○ sp

2.
○ sn
○ sp
○ st

3.
○ sk
○ sm
○ sp

4.
○ sn
○ st
○ sw

5.
○ sn
○ st
○ sw

6.
○ sn
○ st
○ sw

7.
○ sk
○ sm
○ sp

8.
○ sn
○ st
○ sw

9.
○ sk
○ sm
○ sp

Dictation ··

1. ___ ___ile   2. ___ ___ip   3. ___ ___and   4. ___ ___ot

Listen for It

Focus Two consonant sounds said together are called a **consonant blend**. Many words begin with a **consonant + r** blend.

br	cr	dr	fr	gr	pr	tr
bran	**cr**y	**dr**ag	**fr**ee	**gr**ab	**pr**ide	**tr**ip

Say the word for the picture.
Fill in the circle next to the blend you hear at the beginning of the word.

1. 
○ br
○ cr
○ tr

2. 
○ dr
○ gr
○ fr

3. 
○ br
○ tr
○ dr

4. 
○ br
○ cr
○ tr

5. 
○ br
○ cr
○ tr

6. 
○ dr
○ cr
○ tr

7. 
○ dr
○ gr
○ fr

8. 
○ pr
○ gr
○ fr

9. 
○ cr
○ gr
○ fr

Dictation ••

1. ___ ___ab   2. ___ ___ap   3. ___ ___ide   4. ___ ___in

Listen for It

Focus A **consonant blend** has two letters that blend together when you say a word. The letter **l** is the second letter in some blends.

bl	cl	fl	gl	pl	sl
block	**cl**am	**fl**y	**gl**ass	**pl**ane	**sl**ip

Say the word for the picture.
Fill in the circle next to the blend you hear at the beginning of the word.

1.  ○ cl ○ fl ○ pl	2.  ○ cl ○ fl ○ pl	3. ○ bl ○ gl ○ sl
4.  ○ bl ○ gl ○ sl	5. ○ bl ○ cl ○ gl	6. ○ cl ○ fl ○ pl
7.  ○ bl ○ gl ○ sl	8. ○ cl ○ fl ○ pl	9.  ○ cl ○ fl ○ pl

Dictation •

1. _____ _____og   2. _____ _____im   3. _____ _____an   4. _____ _____ip

Write It

Letter Box

| bl | fl | st | cr | sp | dr | gl | gr |

Say the word for the picture.
Write the blend to spell the word. Then read the word.

1. ___ ___ ove	2. ___ ___ amp	3. ___ ___ um
4. ___ ___ op	5. ___ ___ ab	6. ___ ___ ag
7. ___ ___ ill	8. ___ ___ ace	9. ___ ___ ock
10. ___ ___ ue	11. ___ ___ ower	12. ___ ___ aw

Dictation ....

1. _____   2. _____   3. _____   4. _____

Read It

Write the two words that best complete the sentence.

| slim | frog | swim |

1. I can _____ like a _____.

| crab | cross | grab |

2. I _____ the pool and _____ my tube.

| flop | try | fry |

3. I _____ to _____ like a fish.

| stop | step | dry |

4. Then I _____ and get out to _____ off.

| grape | grass | glass |

5. I sip a _____ of cold _____ drink.

Dictation

· ·

_____

Final Consonant Blends
with t, d, p, or k

DAY 1

Listening for Final Consonant Blends: ft, lt, nt, st

Read aloud the focus statement. Then point to the first example and say: *The letters **f** and **t** blend together to make this sound: /ft/. Say /ft/. (/ft/) You hear /ft/ at the end of the word **left**. Say **left**. (left)* Repeat the process for the remaining examples. Then read aloud the directions and call students' attention to number 1. Say: *This picture shows a vest. Say **vest**. (vest) What consonant blend do you hear at the end of **vest**? (/st/) What letters stand for that sound? (st) Fill in the circle next to **st***. Repeat this process for the remaining pictures. **Picture Key:** 1. vest, 2. cent, 3. belt, 4. raft, 5. ghost, 6. nest, 7. salt, 8. tent, 9. gift

Dictation Direct students' attention to the bottom of the page and say:

Listen to each word I say. Then write the letters that stand for the blend you hear at the <u>end</u> of the word.
1. rent 2. lost 3. lift 4. colt 5. test

DAY 2

Writing Final Consonant Blends: ft, lt, nt, st

Direct students' attention to the word box at the top of the page. Guide students in reading each word aloud. Then read aloud the directions and call students' attention to number 1. Say: *The first picture shows a nest. Say **nest**. (nest) What sound do you hear at the end of **nest**? (/st/) Find the word **nest** in the word box and write it on the line.* After students finish writing, ask: *How do you spell **nest**? (n-e-s-t)* Repeat the process for the remaining pictures. **Picture Key:** 1. nest, 2. raft, 3. gift, 4. fist, 5. belt, 6. ant, 7. quilt, 8. tent, 9. cent

Dictation Direct students' attention to the bottom of the page and say:

Listen to each word I say. Then write the letters that stand for the blend you hear at the <u>end</u> of the word.
1. salt 2. fast 3. mint 4. lift 5. bent

DAY 3

Listening for Final Consonant Blends: ld, mp, nd, sk

Read aloud the focus statement. Then point to the first example and say: *The letters **l** and **d** blend together to make this sound: /ld/. Say /ld/. (/ld/) You hear /ld/ at the end of the word **wild**. Say **wild**. (wild)* Repeat the process for the remaining examples. Then read the directions and call students' attention to number 1. Say: *This picture shows a desk. Say **desk**. (desk) What consonant blend do you hear at the end of **desk**? (/sk/) What letters stand for that sound? (sk) Fill in the circle next to **sk***. Repeat this process for the remaining pictures.
Picture Key: 1. desk, 2. stump, 3. hand, 4. pond, 5. cold, 6. lamp, 7. gold, 8. mask, 9. whisk

Dictation Direct students' attention to the bottom of the page and say:

Listen to each word I say. Then write the letters that stand for the blend you hear at the <u>end</u> of the word.
1. camp 2. cold 3. risk 4. bend 5. held

DAY 4

Writing Final Consonant Blends: ld, mp, nd, sk

Direct students' attention to the word box at the top of the page. Guide students in reading each word aloud. Then read aloud the directions and call students' attention to number 1. Say: *The first picture shows a mask. Say **mask**. (mask) What sound do you hear at the end of **mask**? (/sk/) Find the word **mask** in the word box and write it on the line.* After students finish writing, ask: *How do you spell **mask**? (m-a-s-k)* Repeat the process for the remaining pictures.
Picture Key: 1. mask, 2. jump, 3. desk, 4. stamp, 5. gold, 6. sand, 7. lamp, 8. cold, 9. hand

Dictation Direct students' attention to the bottom of the page and say:

Listen to each word I say. Then write the letters that stand for the blend you hear at the <u>end</u> of the word.
1. husk 2. wind 3. bump 4. mold 5. damp

DAY 5

Reading Words with Final Consonant Blends: ft, lt, nt, st, ld, mp, nd, sk

Read aloud the directions and call students' attention to the picture. Say: *This picture shows a swamp. Let's read the first incomplete sentence together: **It was wet and _____ in the _____**. Now let's read the words in the gray bar: **left, cold, swamp**. Which word belongs on the first line? (cold) Write the word **cold** on the first line. Which word completes the sentence: **left** or **swamp**? (swamp) Write the word **swamp** on the next line.* After students finish writing, say: *Now let's read the sentence together: **It was wet and cold in the swamp**.* Repeat this process for the remaining sentences.

Dictation Direct students' attention to the bottom of the page and say:

*Listen to this sentence. Then write it on the line: **We camp in a tent**. (pause) Circle each consonant blend.*

Listen for It

Focus Two consonant sounds said together are called a **consonant blend**. Many words end with a **consonant + t** blend.

ft	lt	nt	st
le**ft**	ti**lt**	mi**nt**	fa**st**

Say the word for the picture.
Fill in the circle next to the blend you hear at the **end** of the word.

1. 	2.	3.
○ nt ○ st ○ lt	○ nt ○ lt ○ ft	○ st ○ nt ○ lt
4. 	5. 	6. 
○ nt ○ st ○ ft	○ st ○ lt ○ nt	○ nt ○ st ○ lt
7.	8. 	9.
○ lt ○ nt ○ st	○ ft ○ st ○ nt	○ st ○ ft ○ lt

Dictation ....

1. re_____   2. lo_____   3. li_____   4. co_____   5. te_____

Name _____

Write It

Word Box

quilt	belt	gift
cent	fist	nest
raft	ant	tent

Write the word that names the picture.

1.

_____

2.

_____

3.

_____

4.

_____

5.

_____

6.

_____

7.

_____

8.

_____

9.

_____

Dictation

1. sa_____   2. fa_____   3. mi_____   4. li_____   5. be_____

Skill: Writing words with final consonant blends   Daily Phonics Practice • EMC 2790 • © Evan-Moor Corp.

Name _____

Listen for It

Focus | Two consonant sounds said together are called a **consonant blend**. Many words end with a consonant blend.

ld	mp	nd	sk
wi**ld**	li**mp**	ba**nd**	a**sk**

Say the word for the picture.
Fill in the circle next to the blend you hear at the **end** of the word.

1. 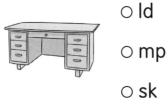 ○ ld ○ mp ○ sk	2.  ○ ld ○ mp ○ nd	3.  ○ sk ○ nd ○ ld
4.  ○ mp ○ ld ○ nd	5.  ○ ld ○ sk ○ nd	6.  ○ mp ○ ld ○ nd
7.  ○ sk ○ ld ○ mp	8.  ○ mp ○ sk ○ nd	9. ○ sk ○ nd ○ mp

Dictation •

1. ca____ ____ 2. co____ ____ 3. ri____ ____ 4. be____ ____ 5. he____ ____

Name _____

Write It

Word Box

cold	stamp	jump
gold	lamp	hand
desk	mask	sand

Write the word that names the picture.

1.

_____

2.

_____

3.

_____

4.

_____

5.

_____

6.

_____

7.

_____

8.

_____

9.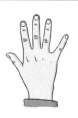

_____

Dictation

1. hu_____ 2. wi_____ 3. bu_____ 4. mo_____ 5. da_____

Read It

Write the two words that best complete the sentence.

> left   cold   swamp

1. It was wet and _____ in the _____.

> soft   felt   sold

2. The moss on the stump _____ _____.

> drift   hunt   pond

3. We saw fog _____ over the _____.

> land   went   lost

4. We _____ west and got _____.

> mist   bent   risk

5. It was a _____ to hike in the _____.

Dictation ···

_____

Initial and Final Consonant Digraphs
ch, sh, th, wh

DAY 1 **Listening for Initial Consonant Digraphs: ch, sh, th, wh**

Read aloud the focus statement. Then point to the first example and say: *The letters **c** and **h** together have this sound: /ch/. Say /ch/.* (/ch/) *You hear /ch/ in the word **chin**. Say **chin**.* (chin) Repeat this process for the remaining examples. For the digraph **wh**, stress the difference between **wh** and **w** by having students first say /w/ and then blow through their lips to say /wh/. Then read the directions and call students' attention to number 1. Say: *This picture shows a chick. Say **chick**.* (chick) *Do you hear /ch/ in **chick**?* (yes) *Fill in the circle.* Repeat this process for the remaining pictures.

Picture Key: Row 1: chick, chain, shoe, chair; Row 2: sky, shell, shovel, cheese; Row 3: tree, three, sheep, thumb; Row 4: whale, whistle, moth, wheel

Dictation   Direct students' attention to the bottom of the page and say:

Listen to each word I say. Then write the letters that stand for the digraph sound you hear at the beginning.
1. chip   2. thin   3. shop   4. while

DAY 2 **Writing Initial Consonant Digraphs: ch, sh, th, wh**

Read aloud the directions and call students' attention to number 1. Say: *Say the number **three**.* (three) *What sound do you hear at the beginning of **three**?* (/th/) *What letters stand for that sound?* (th) *Write the letters **th** on the lines to spell the word **three**.* Repeat the process for the remaining pictures.

Picture Key: 1. three, 2. chin, 3. child, 4. ship, 5. whale, 6. shell, 7. thumb, 8. wheel, 9. chest, 10. sheep

Dictation   Direct students' attention to the bottom of the page and say:

Listen to each word I say. Then write the letters that stand for the <u>first</u> sound you hear.
1. champ   2. thick   3. when   4. shape

DAY 3 **Listening for Final Consonant Digraphs: ch, sh, th**

Read aloud the directions and call students' attention to number 1. Say: *The picture shows money, or cash. Say **cash**.* (cash) *What sound do you hear at the end of **cash**?* (/sh/) *What letters stand for that sound?* (sh) *Write the letters **sh** to complete the word **cash**.* Repeat the process for the remaining pictures.

Picture Key: 1. cash, 2. lunch, 3. path, 4. math, 5. brush, 6. bath, 7. inch, 8. bench, 9. fish

Dictation   Direct students' attention to the bottom of the page and say:

Listen to each word I say. Then write the letters that stand for the digraph sound you hear at the <u>end</u>.
1. push   2. north   3. such   4. crash

DAY 4 **Listening for Initial and Final Consonant Digraphs: ch, sh, th, wh**

Read aloud the directions and call students' attention to number 1. Say: *The picture shows a dish. Say **dish**.* (dish) *Do you hear /sh/ in **dish**?* (yes) *Do you hear /sh/ first or last in **dish**?* (last) *Fill in the second circle.* Repeat the process for the remaining pictures.

Picture Key: 1. dish, 2. north, 3. whistle, 4. chimney, 5. shirt, 6. thermometer, 7. whale, 8. tooth, 9. fish

Dictation   Direct students' attention to the bottom of the page and say:

Listen to each word I say. Then write the letters that stand for the digraph sound you hear at the <u>end</u>.
1. flash   2. munch   3. path   4. moth

DAY 5 **Reading Words with Initial and Final Consonant Digraphs: ch, sh, th, wh**

Direct students' attention to the picture. Say: *This picture shows two children eating tacos. Let's read the first incomplete sentence together: **Have a _____ taco for _____**. Now let's read the words in the gray bar: **lunch, fresh, with**. Which word belongs on the first line?* (fresh) *Write the word **fresh** on the line. Which word completes the sentence: **lunch** or **with**?* (lunch) *Write the word **lunch** on the next line.* After students finish writing, say: *Now let's read the sentence together: **Have a fresh taco for lunch**.* Repeat this process for the remaining sentences.

Dictation   Direct students' attention to the bottom of the page and say:

*Listen to this sentence. Then write it on the line: **A whale is not a fish.***

Name _____

Listen for It

Focus A **digraph** is two letters together that have one new sound. Many words begin with a **consonant + h** digraph.

| ch **ch**in | sh **sh**ake | th **th**in | wh **wh**y |

Say the sound of the digraph. Then say the word for each picture in the row. Fill in the circle under the picture if the word begins with that digraph.

1. **ch-**
   ○   ○   ○   ○

2. **sh-**
   ○   ○   ○   ○

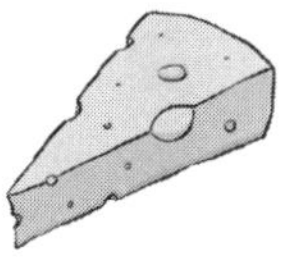

3. **th-**
   ○   ○   ○   ○

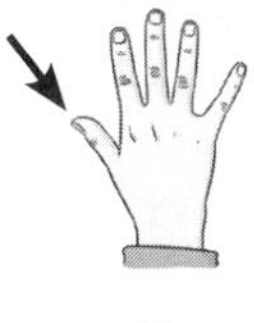

4. **wh-**
   ○   ○   ○   ○

Dictation

1. ___ ___ip   2. ___ ___in   3. ___ ___op   4. ___ ___ile

Write It

Focus   A digraph is two letters together that have one new sound.

Letter Box

ch   sh   th   wh

Say the word for the picture.
Write the digraph to complete the word. Then read the word.

1. ___ ___ ree

6. ___ ___ ell

2. ___ ___ in

7. ___ ___ umb

3. ___ ___ ild

8. ___ ___ eel

4. ___ ___ ip

9. ___ ___ est

5. ___ ___ ale

10.  ___ ___ eep

Dictation ....

1. ___ ___ amp   2. ___ ___ ick   3. ___ ___ en   4. ___ ___ ape

Listen for It

Focus Many words end with a **consonant + h** digraph.

ch	sh	th
mu**ch**	ru**sh**	wi**th**

Say the word for the picture.
Write the digraph to complete the word. Then read the word.

1.

ca___ ___

2.

lun___ ___

3.

pa___ ___

4.

ma___ ___

5.

bru___ ___

6.

ba___ ___

7.

in___ ___

8.

ben___ ___

9.

fi___ ___

Dictation ....

1. pu___ ___   2. nor___ ___   3. su___ ___   4. cra___ ___

Listen for It

Focus   A digraph may begin or end a word.

Say the word for the picture.
Fill in the circle to show if you hear the digraph **first** or **last**.

1.

sh
○——○

2.
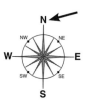
th
○——○

3.

wh
○——○

4.

ch
○——○

5.

sh
○——○

6.

th
○——○

7.

wh
○——○

8.

th
○——○

9.

sh
○——○

Dictation ·

1. fla_____ _____   2. mun_____ _____   3. pa_____ _____   4. mo_____ _____

Read It

Write the two words that best complete the sentence.

> lunch   fresh   with

1. Have a _____ taco for _____.

> which   both   fish

2. We _____ put _____ in our taco.

> crunch   shells   crash

3. I like to _____ on the _____.

> ships   chips   three

4. May I have _____ of your _____?

> dish   white   when

5. I will take your _____ _____ you are done.

Dictation

_____

Initial, Medial, and Final Consonant Digraphs
ck, ng, ph, gh

DAY 1

Listening for Final Consonant Digraphs: ck, ng

Read aloud the focus statement. Then point to the first example and say: *The letters **c** and **k** together have this sound: /k/. Say /k/. (/k/) You hear the /k/ sound at the end of the word **lock**. Say **lock**.* (lock) *Repeat the process for **ng**. Then read the directions and call students' attention to number 1. Say: The picture shows a king. Say **king**.* (king) *What sound do you hear at the end of **king**?* (/ng/) *What letters stand for /ng/?* (ng) *Fill in the circle next to the letters **ng**. Repeat the process for the remaining pictures.*
Picture Key: 1. king, 2. brick, 3. kick, 4. sting, 5. duck, 6. ring, 7. lung, 8. wing, 9. sock

Dictation Direct students' attention to the bottom of the page and say:
Listen to each word I say. Then write the missing digraph. 1. trick 2. bring 3. luck 4. sing

DAY 2

Writing Words with Final Consonant Digraphs: ck, ng

Read aloud the directions and call students' attention to number 1. Say: *The picture shows a lock. Say **lock**.* (lock) *What sound do you hear at the end of **lock**?* (/k/) *Which letters stand for that sound?* (ck) *Write the letters **ck** on the lines to spell the word **lock**. Repeat this process for the remaining pictures.*
Picture Key: 1. lock, 2. swing, 3. truck, 4. kick, 5. brick, 6. hang, 7. wing, 8. sing, 9. clock

Dictation Direct students' attention to the bottom of the page and say:
Listen to each word I say. Then write the missing digraph. 1. rung 2. sick 3. along 4. shack

DAY 3

Listening for Initial, Medial, and Final Consonant Digraphs: ph, gh

Read aloud the focus statement. Then point to the first example and have students say **phone**. Explain: *The /f/ sound you hear in **phone** is spelled with the letters **ph**. Repeat the process for **gh**. Point out that the letters **gh** usually come at the end of a word. Then read aloud the directions and call students' attention to number 1. Say: The picture shows a dolphin. Say **dolphin**.* (dolphin) *Do you hear /f/ in **dolphin**?* (yes) *What letters have the /f/ sound in the word **dolphin**?* (ph) *Underline the letters **ph**. Repeat the process for the remaining words.*

Dictation Direct students' attention to the bottom of the page and say:
Listen to each word I say. Then write the missing digraph. 1. phone 2. tough 3. graph 4. cough

DAY 4

Writing Words with Initial, Medial, and Final Consonant Digraphs: ph, gh

Direct students' attention to the word box at the top of the page. Guide students in reading each word aloud. Then read aloud the directions and call students' attention to number 1. Say: *This picture shows a rock that is rough. Say **rough**.* (rough) *Where do you hear /f/ in **rough**?* (at the end) *Find the word **rough** in the word box and write it on the line. After students finish writing, ask: How do you spell **rough**?* (r-o-u-g-h) *Now underline the letters that have the /f/ sound. Repeat the process for the remaining pictures.*
Picture Key: 1. rough, 2. trophy, 3. graph, 4. photo, 5. laugh, 6. phone, 7. dolphin, 8. gopher, 9. elephant

Dictation Direct students' attention to the bottom of the page and say:
Listen to each word I say. Then write the word on the line. 1. trophy 2. photo 3. rough

DAY 5

Reading Words with Initial and Final Consonant Digraphs: ck, ng, ph, gh

Read the directions and call students' attention to the picture. Say: *This picture shows a team with their trophy. Let's read the first incomplete sentence together: I _____ to the _____ Golf Club. Now let's read the words in the gray bar: **luck, belong, Gophers**. Which word goes on the first line?* (belong) *Write the word **belong** on the first line. Which word completes the sentence: **luck** or **Gophers**?* (Gophers) *Write the word **Gophers** on the next line. After students finish writing, say: Now let's read the sentence together: **I belong to the Gophers Golf Club**. Repeat this process for the remaining sentences.*

Dictation Direct students' attention to the bottom of the page and say:
Listen to this sentence. Then write it on the line: **Did you check the graph?**

Listen for It

Focus The letter pairs **ck** and **ng** are **digraphs**. The **ck** digraph has the /k/ sound. The **ng** digraph has the sound you hear at the end of **ring**. Many words end with these digraphs.

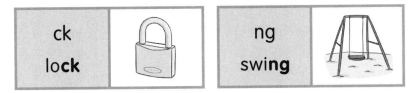

Say the word for the picture.
Fill in the circle next to the digraph you hear at the **end** of the word.

1.
 ○ ck
 ○ ng

2.
 ○ ck
 ○ ng

3.
 ○ ck
 ○ ng

4.
 ○ ck
 ○ ng

5.
 ○ ck
 ○ ng

6.
 ○ ck
 ○ ng

7.
 ○ ck
 ○ ng

8.
 ○ ck
 ○ ng

9.
 ○ ck
 ○ ng

Dictation ···

1. tri_____   2. bri_____   3. lu_____   4. si_____

Write It

Letter Box

ck   ng

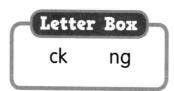

Say the word for the picture and listen to the **final** sound.
Write the digraph that stands for that sound. Then read the word.

1.  lo ___ ___	2. swi ___ ___	3.  tru ___ ___
4.  ki ___ ___	5.  bri ___ ___	6.  ha ___ ___
7.  wi ___ ___	8.  si ___ ___	9.  clo ___ ___

Dictation

1. ru___ ___   2. si___ ___   3. alo___ ___   4. sha___ ___

Skill: Writing words with final consonant digraphs   Daily Phonics Practice • EMC 2790 • © Evan-Moor Corp.

Name _____

Listen for It

Focus A **digraph** is two letters together that have one sound. The digraphs **ph** and **gh** usually have the /f/ sound.

| ph **ph**one | | gh lau**gh** | |

Say the word. Listen to the letter-sounds.
Underline the letters that together have the **/f/** sound.

1.
dolphin

2.
cough

3.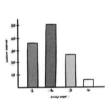
graph

4.
photo

5.
elephant

6.
rough

7.
trophy

8.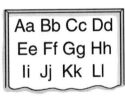
alphabet

9.
gopher

Dictation ....

1. ___ ___one   2. tou___   3. gra___   4. cou___

Name _____

Write It

Day 4 | Week 12

Word Box

dolphin	elephant	gopher
phone	photo	graph
rough	trophy	laugh

Write the word that names the picture.
Underline the letters that together have the **/f/** sound.

1.

_____

2.

_____

3.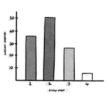

_____

4.

_____

5.

_____

6.

_____

7.

_____

8.

_____

9.

_____

Dictation

1. _____   2. _____   3. _____

Skill: Writing words with consonant digraphs   Daily Phonics Practice • EMC 2790 • © Evan-Moor Corp.

Read It

Write the two words that best complete the sentence.

> luck   belong   Gophers

1. I _____ to the _____ Golf Club.

> laugh   sting   tough

2. We _____ and have fun, but we play _____.

> long   lock   whack

3. I can _____ the ball a _____ way!

> trick   trophy   Jack

4. In the last game, _____ won a _____.

> phone   photo   graph

5. Mom took a _____ with her _____.

Dictation

_____

DAY 1

Listening for Words with Variant Spellings

Read aloud the focus statement. Then point to the first example and say: *The letters t, c, and h blend together to make this sound: /ch/. Say /ch/.* (/ch/) *You hear /ch/ at the end of the word* **watch**. *Say* **watch**. (watch) Repeat the process for **dge**. Then read aloud the directions and call students' attention to number 1. Say: *This is a crutch. Say* **crutch**. (crutch) *What sound do you hear at the end of* **crutch**? (/ch/) *What letters have that sound?* (tch) *Fill in the circle next to* **tch**. Repeat this process for the remaining pictures.
Picture Key: 1. crutch, 2. hedge, 3. fudge, 4. patch, 5. bridge, 6. hatch, 7. fetch, 8. match, 9. judge

Dictation Direct students' attention to the bottom of the page and say:
Listen to each word I say. Then write the letters that stand for the sound you hear at the end of the word.
1. batch   2. stitch   3. edge   4. smudge

DAY 2

Listening for Words with Variant Spellings

Read aloud the directions and call students' attention to number 1. Say: *The picture shows an animal called a badger. Say* **badger**. (badger) *Do you hear /j/ in* **badger**? (yes) *Do you hear /j/ at the beginning, in the middle, or at the end of* **badger**? (middle) *Fill in the middle circle.* Repeat the process for the remaining pictures.
Picture Key: 1. badger, 2. switch, 3. kitchen, 4. badge, 5. watch, 6. pitcher, 7. catcher, 8. bridge, 9. crutch, 10. fetch, 11. match, 12. fudge

Dictation Direct students' attention to the bottom of the page and say:
Listen to each word I say. Then write the missing letters.   *1. clutch   2. lodge   3. switch   4. dodge*

DAY 3

Writing Words with Variant Spellings

Read aloud the directions and call students' attention to number 1. Say: *The picture shows a latch on a gate. Say* **latch**. (latch) *What sound do you hear at the end of* **latch**? (/ch/) *What letters have that sound?* (tch) *Write the letters* **tch** *on the line to spell the word* **latch**. Repeat the process for the remaining pictures.
Picture Key: 1. latch, 2. wedge, 3. badge, 4. judge, 5. watches, 6. catcher, 7. pitcher, 8. kitchen, 9. bridge

Dictation Direct students' attention to the bottom of the page and say:
Listen to each word I say. Then write the missing letters.   *1. hitch   2. dodge   3. notch   4. ridge*

DAY 4

Writing Words with Variant Spellings

Direct students' attention to the word box at the top of the page. Guide students in reading each word aloud. Then read aloud the directions and call students' attention to number 1. Say: *The first picture shows a crutch. Say* **crutch**. (crutch) *What sound do you hear at the end of* **crutch**? (/ch/) *Find the word* **crutch** *in the word box and write it on the line.* After students finish writing, ask: *How do you spell* **crutch**? (c-r-u-t-c-h) Repeat the process for the remaining pictures.
Picture Key: 1. crutch, 2. badge, 3. kitchen, 4. bridge, 5. watch, 6. fetch, 7. badger, 8. pitcher, 9. fudge

Dictation Direct students' attention to the bottom of the page and say:
Listen to each word I say. Then write the word that you hear.   *1. hedge   2. latch   3. catch*

DAY 5

Reading Words with Variant Spellings

Direct students' attention to the picture. Say: *This picture shows a boy eating fudge. Let's read the first incomplete sentence together:* **Rosa made a _____ of _____.** *Now let's read the words in the gray bar:* **batch, match, fudge.** *Which word belongs on the first line?* (batch) *Write the word* **batch** *on the first line. Which word completes the sentence?* (fudge) *Write the word* **fudge** *on the next line.* After students finish writing, say: *Now let's read the sentence together:* **Rosa made a batch of fudge.** Repeat this process for the remaining sentences.

Dictation Direct students' attention to the bottom of the page and say:
Listen to this sentence. Then write it on the line: **He made a sketch of the bridge.**

Listen for It

The letters **tch** have the /ch/ sound. The letters **dge** have the /j/ sound. Both **tch** and **dge** are usually at the end of a word.

| tch
wa**tch** | | dge
ba**dge** | |

Say the word for the picture.
Fill in the circle next to the letters that stand for the **final** sound you hear.

1.  ○ tch ○ dge	2.  ○ tch ○ dge	3.  ○ tch ○ dge
4.  ○ tch ○ dge	5.  ○ tch ○ dge	6. ○ tch ○ dge
7.  ○ tch ○ dge	8. ○ tch ○ dge	9.  ○ tch ○ dge

Dictation ....

1. ba_____   2. sti_____   3. e_____   4. smu_____

Listen for It

Say the sound of the letters. Then say the word for the picture.
Fill in the circle to show if you hear the sound **first**, in the **middle**, or **last**.

1.

dge
○──────○──────○

2.

tch
○──────○──────○

3.
 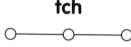

tch
○──────○──────○

4.

dge
○──────○──────○

5.

tch
○──────○──────○

6.
 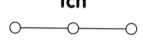

tch
○──────○──────○

7.

tch
○──────○──────○

8.

dge
○──────○──────○

9.
  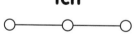

tch
○──────○──────○

10.

tch
○──────○──────○

11.

tch
○──────○──────○

12.

dge
○──────○──────○

Dictation

1. clu_____   2. lo_____   3. swi_____   4. do_____

Write It

tch   dge

Say the word for the picture and listen to the letter-sounds.
Write the letters that stand for that sound. Then read the word.

1.  la_____	2. we_____	3. ba_____
4.  ju_____	5. wa_____es	6.  ca_____er
7. pi_____er	8.  ki_____en	9.  bri_____

Dictation

1. hi_____   2. do_____   3. no_____   4. ri_____

Write It

Word Box

badge	badger	crutch
fetch	kitchen	watch
fudge	pitcher	bridge

Write the word that names the picture.

1.

_____

2.

_____

3.

_____

4.

_____

5.

_____

6.

_____

7.

_____

8.

_____

9.

_____

Dictation

1. _____   2. _____   3. _____

Read It

Write the two words that best complete the sentence.

| batch | match | fudge |

1. Rosa made a _____ of _____.

| watch | badge | kitchen |

2. She let me sit in the _____ and _____.

| fetch | hutch | bridge |

3. I had to _____ salt from the _____.

| fridge | pitcher | patch |

4. Rosa got a _____ from the _____.

| wedge | fudge | edge |

5. I cut a _____ from the _____ of the pan.

Dictation •

_____

Long a Vowel Digraphs
ai, ay

DAY 1

Listening for Long a Digraphs

Read aloud the focus statement. Then point to the first example and say: *The vowels **a** and **i** together have the **long a** sound you hear in **rain**. Say **rain**.* (rain) Repeat the process for the vowels **a** and **y** in **hay**. Then read the directions and call students' attention to number 1. Say: *The picture shows two envelopes, or some mail. Say **mail**.* (mail) *Where do you hear /ā/ in **mail**?* (in the middle) *Which letters have the **long a** sound?* (ai) *Underline the letters **ai** in **mail**.* Repeat the process for the remaining words.

Dictation Direct students' attention to the bottom of the page and say:
Listen to each word I say. Write the word that you hear.
1. play   2. mail (as in a letter you send)   3. brain   4. hay

DAY 2

Writing Words with Long a Digraphs

Read aloud the directions and call students' attention to number 1. Say: *This picture shows rain. Where do you hear /ā/ in **rain**?* (in the middle) *Which two letters usually spell the **long a** sound in the middle of a word?* (ai) *Write **ai** on the line to complete the word. Now let's read it together: **rain**.* Repeat the process for the remaining pictures.

Picture Key: 1. rain, 2. hay, 3. tray, 4. nail, 5. spray, 6. snail, 7. sail, 8. train, 9. pay, 10. X-ray, 11. tail, 12. paint

Dictation Direct students' attention to the bottom of the page and say:
Listen to each word I say. Write the word that you hear.   *1. pail   2. gray   3. fail   4. say*

DAY 3

Writing Words with Long a Digraphs

Direct students' attention to the word box at the top of the page. Guide students in reading each word aloud. Then read aloud the directions and call students' attention to number 1. Say: *The picture shows a nail. Say **nail**.* (nail) *Where do you hear /ā/ in **nail**?* (in the middle) *Find the word **nail** in the word box and write it on the line.* After students finish writing, ask: *How do you spell **nail**?* (n-a-i-l) Repeat the process for the remaining pictures.

Picture Key: 1. nail, 2. spray, 3. braid, 4. pay, 5. rain, 6. train, 7. sail, 8. brain, 9. hay, 10. trail, 11. tray, 12. mail

Dictation Direct students' attention to the bottom of the page and say:
Listen to each word I say. Write the word that you hear.   *1. paint   2. stay   3. clay   4. pain (as in hurt)*

DAY 4

Writing Words with Long a Digraphs

Direct students' attention to the word box at the top of the page. Guide students in reading each word aloud. Then read aloud the directions and call students' attention to number 1. Say: *Let's read the incomplete sentence together: **A brush is used to _____**. Which word from the box best completes the sentence?* (paint) *Yes, a brush is used to paint. Write **paint** on the line.* After students finish writing, say: *Now let's read the sentence together: **A brush is used to paint**.* Repeat this process for the remaining sentences.

Dictation Direct students' attention to the bottom of the page and say:
Listen to this sentence. Then write it on the line: **She will paint the tray.**

DAY 5

Reading Words with Long a Digraphs

Read aloud the directions and call students' attention to the picture. Say: *This picture shows a subway station. Let's read the first incomplete sentence together: **This is the _____ to the _____**. Now let's read the words in the gray bar: **subway, wait, way**. Which word belongs on the first line?* (way) *Write **way** on the first line. Which word should you write on the second line?* (subway) *Write **subway** on the line.* After students have finished writing, say: *Now let's read the sentence together: **This is the way to the subway**.* Repeat this process for the remaining sentences.

Dictation Direct students' attention to the bottom of the page and say:
Listen to this sentence. Then write it on the line: **We will sail away today.**

Name _____

Listen for It

Focus A **digraph** is two letters together that have one sound. The letter pairs **ai** and **ay** are **vowel digraphs** that have the **long a** sound, /ā/. Usually, **ai** is in the middle of a word and **ay** is at the end of a word.

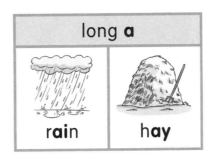

long **a**

r**ai**n

h**ay**

Say the word. Listen to the letter-sounds.
Underline the two letters that together have the **long a** sound.

1. mail	2. clay	3.  May
4. paint	5. jail	6. brain
7. play	8. nail	9. chain

Dictation •

1. _____   2. _____   3. _____   4. _____

Write It

Letter Box

ai   ay

Write **ai** or **ay** to complete the word. Read the word.

1.  r ___ n	2.  h ___	3. tr ___
4. n ___ l	5. spr ___	6. sn ___ l
7. s ___ l	8.  tr ___ n	9. p ___
10. 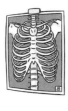 X-r ___	11.  t ___ l	12. p ___ nt

Dictation

1. _____   2. _____   3. _____   4. _____

Daily Phonics Practice • EMC 2790 • © Evan-Moor Corp.

Write It

Word Box

sail	tray	braid	trail	spray	brain
pay	rain	mail	nail	hay	train

Write the word that names the picture.

1. _____	2. _____	3. _____
4. _____	5. _____	6. _____
7. _____	8. _____	9. _____
10.  _____	11. _____	12. _____

Dictation

1. _____   2. _____   3. _____   4. _____

Skill: Writing words with **long a** digraphs   **85**

Name _____

Write It

Word Box

play	gray	snail	runway
trail	paint	clay	brain

Write the word that best completes the sentence clue.

1. A brush is used to _____.

2. You use your _____ to think.

3. A _____ has a shell to keep it safe.

4. People act out a _____ on a stage.

5. A plane lands on a long _____.

6. You can shape things out of _____.

7. A snail makes a _____ of slime.

8. The sky is _____ when it rains.

Dictation •

_____

Read It

Write the two words that best complete the sentence.

| subway | wait | way |

1. This is the _____ to the _____.

| may | wait | train |

2. We will _____ for the next _____.

| pay | stay | sail |

3. I must _____ in this line to _____.

| today | away | may |

4. The train _____ be late _____.

| rain | anyway | delay |

5. I hope the _____ does not _____ us.

Dictation •

_____

Long e Vowel Digraphs
ee, ea, ey, ie

DAY 1

Listening for Long e: ee, ea

Read aloud the focus statement. Then point to the first example and say: *Two e's together have the* **long e** *sound: /ē/. You hear /ē/ in* **feet**. *Say* **feet**. (feet) Repeat the process for the vowels **e** and **a** in **leaf**. Then read aloud the directions and call students' attention to number 1. Say: *Point to the jeep. Say* **jeep**. (jeep) *Do you hear /ē/ in* **jeep**? (yes) *What letters have the* **long e** *sound?* (ee) *Underline the letters* **ee** *in* **jeep**. Repeat the process for the remaining words.

Dictation Direct students' attention to the bottom of the page and say:

Listen to each word I say. Then write the missing letters to complete the word.   1. green   2. treat   3. sleep

DAY 2

Listening for Long e: ey, ie

Read aloud the focus statement. Then point to the first example and say: *The letters* **e** *and* **y** *together have the* **long e** *sound at the end of* **donkey**. *Say* **donkey**. (donkey) Repeat for the vowels **i** and **e** in **chief**. Then read the directions and call students' attention to number 1. Say: *The picture shows someone playing hockey. Say* **hockey**. (hockey) *Do you hear /ē/ in* **hockey**? (yes) *What letters have the* **long e** *sound?* (ey) *Underline the letters* **ey** *in* **hockey**. Repeat the process for the remaining words. For the words **monkey**, **money**, and **honey**, you may want to point out the variant pronunciation of the **short u** sound for the letter **o**.

Dictation Direct students' attention to the bottom of the page and say:

Listen to each word I say. Then write the missing letters to complete the word.   1. field   2. chimney   3. chief

DAY 3

Writing Words with Long e Digraphs: ee, ea, ey, ie

Direct students' attention to the word box at the top of the page. Guide students in reading each word aloud. Then read aloud the directions and call students' attention to number 1. Say: *The first picture shows an eagle. Say* **eagle**. *Where do you hear /ē/ in* **eagle**? (at the beginning) *Find the word* **eagle** *in the word box and write it on the line.* After students finish writing, ask: *How do you spell* **eagle**? (e-a-g-l-e) Repeat the process for the remaining pictures.

Picture Key: 1. eagle, 2. three, 3. hockey, 4. teach, 5. field, 6. key, 7. tea, 8. jeep, 9. piece, 10. feet, 11. read, 12. money

Dictation Direct students' attention to the bottom of the page and say:

Listen to this sentence. Then write it on the line: **I have the key to the jeep.**

DAY 4

Writing Words with Long e Digraphs: ee, ea, ey, ie

Direct students' attention to the word box at the top of the page. Guide students in reading each word aloud. Then read aloud the directions and call students' attention to number 1. Say: *Let's read the clue together:* **This tastes sweet.** *Which word from the box best names something that is sweet?* (honey) *Yes, honey is sweet. Write* **honey** *on the line.* Repeat this process for the remaining clues.

Dictation Direct students' attention to the bottom of the page and say:

Listen to this sentence. Then write it on the line: **I like to read about hockey.**

DAY 5

Reading Words with Long e Digraphs: ee, ea, ey, ie

Read aloud the directions and call students' attention to the picture. Say: *This picture shows a donkey watching bees make honey. Let's read the first incomplete sentence together:* **Bees like this _____ because it is _____.** *Now let's read the words in the gray bar:* **field, speed, green.** *Which word belongs on the first line?* (field) *Write* **field** *on the first line. Which word completes the sentence,* **speed** *or* **green**? (green) *Write* **green** *on the line.* After students have finished writing, say: *Now let's read the sentence together:* **Bees like this field because it is green.** Repeat this process for the remaining sentences.

Dictation Direct students' attention to the bottom of the page and say:

Listen to this sentence. Then write it on the line: **Do not let the thief steal my money!**

Name _____

Listen for It

Focus The vowel pairs **ee** and **ea** are digraphs that often have the **long e** sound.

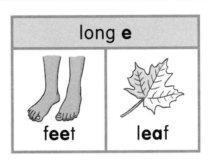

long **e**

fe**ee**t | l**ea**f

Say the word. Underline the two letters that together have the **long e** sound.

1.  jeep	2. peach	3. wheel
4. eagle	5. sneeze	6. peek
7. queen	8. cheek	9. wheat

Dictation ··

1. ___ ___ ee ___   2. ___ ___ ea ___   3. ___ ___ ee ___

Listen for It

Focus The vowel digraphs **ey** and **ie** often have the **long e** sound.
The digraph **ey** is usually at the end of a word.
The digraph **ie** is usually in the middle of a word.

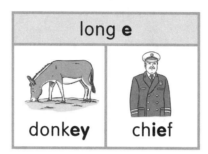

long **e**

donk**ey**   chi**e**f

Say the word. Underline the two letters that together have the **long e** sound.

1. hockey	2. monkey	3. thief
4. piece	5. key	6. field
7. turkey	8. money	9. honey

Dictation ●

1. ___ ie ___ ___   2. ___ ___ ___ ___ ___ ey   3. ___ ___ ie ___

Name _____

Write It

Word Box

| hockey | money | piece | field | teach | three |
| read | eagle | feet | tea | jeep | key |

Write the word that names the picture.

1.

_____

2.

_____

3.

_____

4.

_____

5.

_____

6.

_____

7.

_____

8.

_____

9.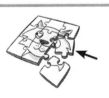

_____

10.

_____

11.

_____

12.

_____

Dictation

_____

Skill: Writing words with **long e** digraphs   **91**

Write It

Word Box

donkey	hockey	sleep	honey
jeep	chief	field	read

Write the word that fits the clue.

1. This tastes sweet. _____

2. This has four wheels. _____

3. This has a lot of grass. _____

4. This has four legs. _____

5. You do this in bed. _____

6. You do this with a book. _____

7. This is a game. _____

8. This is a job for a leader. _____

Dictation ....

_____

Read It

Write the two words that best complete the sentence.

| field | speed | green |

1. Bees like this _____ because it is _____.

| leaf | sweet | honey |

2. The bees make _____ that is _____.

| treat | money | donkey |

3. The _____ wants to eat a _____.

| thief | reach | clean |

4. Will he be a _____ and _____ into the hive?

| steal | teach | piece |

5. The bees will _____ the donkey not to _____!

Dictation •••

_____

Long i Vowel Patterns
ie, igh

DAY 1 · **Listening for Long i**

Read aloud the focus statement. Then point to the first example and say: *We've just learned that the letters i and e together in a word can stand for the **long e** sound. But the letters i and e can also stand for the **long i** sound you hear in the word **tie**. Say **tie**.* (tie) Then point to the word **bright** and say: *The letters **i**, **g**, and **h** together can also have the **long i** sound. Say **bright**.* (bright) Then read the directions and call students' attention to number 1. Say: *The picture shows a light. Say **light**.* (light) *Do you hear /ī/ in **light**?* (yes) *What letters have the **long i** sound?* (igh) *Underline the letters **igh** in **light**.* Repeat the process for the remaining words.

Dictation Direct students' attention to the bottom of the page and say:

Listen to each word I say. Then write the missing letters to complete the word. 1. *lied* 2. *high* 3. *flight* 4. *spies*

DAY 2 · **Writing Words with the Sound of Long i**

Direct students' attention to the word box at the top of the page. Guide students in reading each word aloud. Then read aloud the directions and call students' attention to number 1. Say: *The picture shows a tie. Find the word **tie** in the word box and write it on the line.* After students finish writing, ask: *How do you spell **tie**?* (t-i-e) Repeat the process for the remaining pictures.
Picture Key: 1. tie, 2. tights, 3. fight, 4. light, 5. tied, 6. fries, 7. night, 8. spies, 9. thigh, 10. pie, 11. cries, 12. flies

Dictation Direct students' attention to the bottom of the page and say:

Listen to this sentence. Then write it on the line: **She cries at night.**

DAY 3 · **Reading Words with the Sound of Long i**

Read aloud the directions and call students' attention to number 1. Ask: *What does the picture show?* (a light) *Which word spells **light**?* (l-i-g-h-t) *Fill in the circle next to the word **light**. What letters have the **long i** sound in **light**?* (igh) Repeat the process for the remaining words.

Dictation Direct students' attention to the bottom of the page and say:

Listen to this sentence. Then write it on the line: **A bat flies at night.**

DAY 4 · **Writing Words with the Sound of Long i**

Direct students' attention to the word box at the top of the page. Guide students in reading each word aloud. Then read aloud the directions and call students' attention to number 1. Say: *Let's read the clue:* **This is part of your leg.** *Which word from the box names a part of your leg?* (thigh) *Yes, write **thigh** on the line.* Repeat the process for the remaining clues.

Dictation Direct students' attention to the bottom of the page and say:

Listen to this sentence. Then write it on the line: **I eat pie at night.**

DAY 5 · **Reading Words with the Sound of Long i**

Read aloud the directions and call students' attention to the picture. Say: *This picture shows a bird flying away from her baby birds in a nest. Let's read the first incomplete sentence together:* **There is a _____ to see _____ in the tree.** *Now let's read the words in the gray bar:* **high, sight, skies.** *Which word belongs on the first line?* (sight) *Write **sight** on the first line. Which word completes the sentence, **high** or **skies**?* (high) *Write **high** on the line.* After students have finished writing, say: *Now let's read the sentence together:* **There is a sight to see high in the tree.** Repeat this process for the remaining sentences.

Dictation Direct students' attention to the bottom of the page and say:

Listen to this sentence. Then write it on the line: **The bright sun is high in the sky.**

Listen for It

Focus   The letters **ie** and **igh** can stand for the **long i** sound.

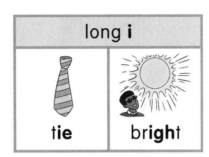

| long i |
| tie | br**igh**t |

Say the word. Underline the letters that together have the **long i** sound.

1.
light

2.
pie

3.
cries

4.
tied

5.
night

6.
flies

7.
high

8.
fries

9.
fight

Dictation •

1. ___ ie ___   2. ___ igh   3. ___ ___ igh ___   4. ___ ___ ie ___

Write It

Word Box

cries	tied	fries	fight	spies	pie
tights	thigh	light	tie	night	flies

Write the word that names the picture.

1.

_____

2.

_____

3.

_____

4.

_____

5.

_____

6.

_____

7.

_____

8.

_____

9.

_____

10.

_____

11.

_____

12.

_____

Dictation •

_____

Read It

Fill in the circle next to the word that names the picture.

1.  ○ lie ○ light	2.  ○ sighs ○ pies	3. ○ tied ○ night
4.  ○ high ○ sigh	5.  ○ spies ○ sight	6.  ○ fright ○ fries
7.  ○ bright ○ might	8.  ○ thighs ○ cries	9. ○ fight ○ night
10.  ○ tights ○ flies	11. ○ fight ○ fries	12. ○ tie ○ tight

Dictation

•••

_____

Write It

Word Box

light	right	night	thigh
flies	pie	high	tie

Write the word that fits the clue.

1. This is part of your leg. _____

2. You can do this with a rope. _____

3. This is sweet to eat. _____

4. If you do not go left, you go this way. _____

5. This helps you see at night. _____

6. A tall tree is this. _____

7. When it is not day, it is this. _____

8. These are bugs that fly. _____

Dictation

_____

_____

Read It

Write the two words that best complete the sentence.

high   sight   skies

1. There is a _____ to see _____ in the tree.

flight   tried   might

2. The baby birds _____ go into _____.

flies   night   fright

3. The mom _____ away at _____ to get food.

fight   right   tries

4. She _____ to find the _____ food for her babies.

cries   bright   daylight

5. When _____ comes, the _____ will stop.

Dictation •

_____

Long o Vowel Digraphs
oa, ow, oe

DAY 1 **Listening for Long o**

Read aloud the focus statement. Then point to the first example and say: *The letters **o** and **a** together in a word usually have the **long o** sound: /ō/. You hear the **long o** sound in **goat**. Say **goat**.* (goat) Repeat the process for **bow** and **toe**, pointing out that these spellings of the **long o** sound are less common and often stand for other vowel sounds as well. Then read aloud the directions and call students' attention to number 1. Say: *The picture shows a **doe**. Say **doe**.* (doe) *What letters have the **long o** sound in **doe**?* (oe) *Underline the letters **oe** in **doe**.* Repeat the process for the remaining words. For number 4, be sure to point out that the word **tow** has the same sound as the word **toe**, but a different spelling and meaning.

Dictation Direct students' attention to the bottom of the page and say:

Listen to each word I say. Then write the missing letters to complete the word.   1. road   2. foe   3. loan   4. snow

DAY 2 **Writing Words with Long o Digraphs**

Direct students' attention to the word box at the top of the page. Guide students in reading each word aloud. Then read aloud the directions and call students' attention to number 1. Say: *The picture shows pieces of toast. Say **toast**.* (toast) *Find the word **toast** in the word box and write it on the line.* After students finish writing, ask: *How do you spell **toast**?* (t-o-a-s-t) Repeat the process for the remaining pictures.
Picture Key: 1. toast, 2. toe, 3. toad, 4. mow, 5. crow, 6. road, 7. shadow, 8. loaf, 9. doe, 10. throw, 11. banjoes, 12. boat

Dictation Direct students' attention to the bottom of the page and say:

Listen to this sentence. Then write it on the line: **We see a crow on the road.**

DAY 3 **Reading Words with Long o Digraphs**

Read aloud the directions and call students' attention to number 1. Say: *The picture shows an oak tree. Say **oak**.* (oak) *Which word spells **oak**?* (o-a-k) *What letters have the **long o** sound in **oak**?* (oa) *Fill in the circle next to the word **oak**.* Repeat the process for the remaining words.

Dictation Direct students' attention to the bottom of the page and say:

Listen to this sentence. Then write it on the line: **Mow the grass by the oak.**

DAY 4 **Writing Words with Long o Digraphs**

Direct students' attention to the word box at the top of the page. Guide students in reading each word aloud. Then read aloud the directions and call students' attention to number 1. Say: *Let's read the clue:* **This is something you eat.** *Which word from the box names a food?* (oatmeal) *Yes, oatmeal is something you eat. Write **oatmeal** on the line.* Repeat this process for the remaining clues.

Dictation Direct students' attention to the bottom of the page and say:

Listen to this sentence. Then write it on the line: **Does a toad grow toes?**

DAY 5 **Reading Words with Long o Digraphs**

Read aloud the directions and call students' attention to the picture. Say: *This picture shows a rainbow over a hay field. Let's read the first incomplete sentence together:* **The ____ wants the hay to ____.** *Now let's read the words in the gray bar:* **grow, coat, goat.** *Which word belongs on the first line?* (goat) *Write **goat** on the first line. Which word completes the sentence, **grow** or **coat**?* (grow) *Write **grow** on the line.* After students have finished writing, say: *Now let's read the sentence together:* **The goat wants the hay to grow.** Repeat this process for the remaining sentences.

Dictation Direct students' attention to the bottom of the page and say:

Listen to this sentence. Then write it on the line: **Show me that coat.**

Listen for It

Focus The vowel pair **oa** is a digraph that usually has the **long o** sound. The digraphs **ow** and **oe** can also have the **long o** sound.

goa**t**

bow

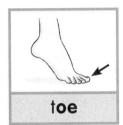

toe

Say the word. Underline the two letters that together have the **long o** sound.

1.  doe	2.  bowl	3.  loaf
4. tow	5. hoe	6.  float
7.  banjoes	8.  rainbow	9. oatmeal

Dictation •

1. ___ oa ___   2. ___ oe   3. ___ oa ___   4. ___ ___ ow

Write It

Word Box

mow	boat	loaf	toast	banjoes	road
toad	crow	throw	doe	shadow	toe

Write the word that names the picture.

1.

_____

2.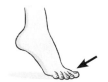

_____

3.

_____

4.

_____

5.

_____

6.

_____

7.

_____

8.

_____

9.

_____

10.

_____

11.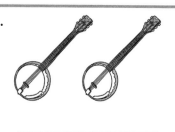

_____

12.

_____

Dictation

···

_____

Name _____

Read It

Fill in the circle next to the word that names the picture.

1.  ○ oak　○ rake	2.  ○ mow　○ may	3. ○ blow　○ bow
4. 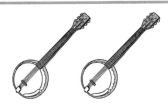 ○ banjoes　○ shadows	5. ○ taste　○ toast	6. ○ crow　○ cry
7. ○ grow　○ doe	8.  ○ bow　○ bowl	9.  ○ flown　○ float
10.  ○ read　○ road	11.  ○ row　○ roam	12.  ○ three　○ throw

Dictation

● ●

_____

Write It

Word Box

float	pillow	grow	rainbow
toad	oatmeal	throw	toes

Write the word that fits the clue.

1. This is something you eat. _____

2. This is something on a bed. _____

3. You have ten of these. _____

4. A boat can do this. _____

5. A plant can do this. _____

6. This is like a frog. _____

7. You do this with a ball. _____

8. You can see this in the sky. _____

Dictation •••

_____

Read It

Write the two words that best complete the sentence.

> grow   coat   goat

1. The _____ wants the hay to _____.

> rainbow   low   toast

2. The _____ is _____ in the sky.

> bowl   goes   road

3. The _____ _____ over the hill.

> blows   glows   oak

4. The wind _____ the _____ tree.

> flown   crows   doe

5. Some _____ have _____ away.

Dictation

_____

Long u Vowel Digraphs
ue, ew, ui

DAY 1 — **Listening for Long u**

Read aloud the focus statement. Then point to the first example and say: *The vowels **u** and **e** together usually have the **long u** sound: /ū/. We hear /ū/ in **clue**. Say **clue**.* (clue) Repeat the process for the letters **e** and **w** in **grew** and **u** and **i** in **fruit**. Then read aloud the directions and call students' attention to number 1. Say: *The picture shows a tree that the wind blew. Say **blew**.* (blew) *Do you hear /ū/ in **blew**?* (yes) *What letters have the **long u** sound?* (ew) *Underline the letters **ew** in **blew**.* Point out that the word **blew** is a homophone of the word **b-l-u-e**, as in the color **blue**. Remind students that homophones are words that sound alike but have different spellings and meanings. Then continue guiding students through the words.

Dictation Direct students' attention to the bottom of the page and say:

Listen to each word I say. Then write the missing letters to complete the word. 1. true 2. chew 3. stew 4. duel

DAY 2 — **Reading Words with Long u Digraphs**

Read the directions and call students' attention to number 1. Say: *Let's read the phrase together: **sticky glue**. Which word has the **long u** sound?* (glue) *Underline the word **glue**. Then draw a line to the picture that shows a bottle of glue.* Repeat this process for the remaining phrases.

Dictation Direct students' attention to the bottom of the page and say:

Listen to each word I say. Then write the missing letters to complete the word. 1. brew 2. clue 3. drew 4. cruel

DAY 3 — **Writing Words with Long u Digraphs**

Direct students' attention to the word box at the top of the page. Guide students in reading each word aloud. Then read aloud the directions and call students' attention to number 1. Say: *The picture shows a calendar with Tuesday circled. Say **Tuesday**.* (Tuesday) *Find the word **Tuesday** in the word box and write it on the line.* After students finish writing, ask: *How do you spell **Tuesday**?* (T-u-e-s-d-a-y) Repeat the process for the remaining pictures.

Picture Key: 1. Tuesday, 2. threw, 3. glue, 4. fuel, 5. news, 6. fruit, 7. rescue, 8. suit, 9. clue, 10. chew, 11. flew, 12. screw

Dictation Direct students' attention to the bottom of the page and say:

*Listen to this sentence. Then write it on the line: **We flew to his rescue.***

DAY 4 — **Writing Words with Long u Digraphs**

Direct students' attention to the word box at the top of the page. Guide students in reading each word aloud. Then read aloud the directions and call students' attention to number 1. Say: *Let's read the clue: **You use your teeth to do this**. Which word from the box means something you do with your teeth?* (chew) *Yes, you chew with your teeth. Write **chew** on the line.* Repeat this process for the remaining clues.

Dictation Direct students' attention to the bottom of the page and say:

*Listen to this sentence. Then write it on the line: **We made stew on Tuesday.***

DAY 5 — **Reading Words with Long u Digraphs**

Read aloud the directions and call students' attention to the picture. Say: *This picture shows a forest fire. Let's read the first incomplete sentence together: **A big fire was in the _____ last _____**. Now let's read the words in the gray bar: **news, clue, Tuesday**. Which word belongs on the first line?* (news) *Write **news** on the first line. Which word completes the sentence, **clue** or **Tuesday**?* (Tuesday) *Write the word **Tuesday** on the next line.* After students finish writing, say: *Now let's read the sentence together: **A big fire was in the news last Tuesday**.* Repeat this process for the remaining sentences.

Dictation Direct students' attention to the bottom of the page and say:

*Listen to this sentence. Then write it on the line: **The blue jewel was a clue.***

Listen for It

Focus The letter pairs **ue**, **ew**, and **ui** are digraphs that usually have the **long u** sound.

cl**ue**

gr**ew**

fr**ui**t

Say the word. Underline the two letters that together have the **long u** sound.

1.
blew

2.
glue

3.
chew

4.
juice

5.
suit

6.
news

7.
fuel

8.
flew

9.
rescue

Dictation •

1. ___ ___ ue   2. ___ ___ ew   3. ___ ___ ew   4. ___ ue ___

Read It

Read the phrase. Underline the word or words that have the **long u** sound.
Then draw a line to the correct picture.

1. sticky glue

2. flew high in the sky

3. men in suits

4. fuel for a car

5. read the news

6. a rescued boy

7. a Tuesday in June

8. a jewel on a ring

Dictation

1. ___ ___ ew   2. ___ ___ ue   3. ___ ___ ew   4. ___ ___ ue ___

Name _____

Write It

Word Box

suit	chew	clue	flew	fuel	glue
fruit	news	rescue	screw	threw	Tuesday

Write the word that names the picture.

1.

_____

2.

_____

3.

_____

4.

_____

5.

_____

6.

_____

7.

_____

8.

_____

9.

_____

10.

_____

11.

_____

12.

_____

Dictation

•••

_____

Name _____

Write It

Word Box

fuel	chew	jewel	glue
Tuesday	suits	blew	stew

Write the word that fits the clue.

1. You use your teeth to do this. _____

2. This sticks to things. _____

3. This can be red, blue, or green. _____

4. This is something you eat. _____

5. A car needs this. _____

6. This is a day of the week. _____

7. This can be something the wind did. _____

8. Men wear these. _____

Dictation ••

_____

Read It

Write the two words that best complete the sentence.

| news | clue | Tuesday |

1. A big fire was in the _____ last _____.

| jewel | grew | blew |

2. The wind _____, and the fire _____.

| rescue | drew | crew |

3. A brave _____ came to the _____.

| blue | true | few |

4. It is _____ that the fire was out in a _____ days.

| blue | stew | flew |

5. The sky became _____, and the birds _____ back.

Dictation

_____

_____

R-Controlled Vowels
ar, or, er, ir, ur, air, are, ear

DAY 1
Listening for R-Controlled Vowels: ar, or

Read aloud the focus statement. Then point to the first example and say: *The letters **a** and **r** together can have this sound: /âr/. Say /âr/. (/âr/) You hear /âr/ in **dart**. Say **dart**.* (dart) Point to the second example and say: *The letters **o** and **r** blend together to have this sound: /ôr/. Say /ôr/. (/ôr/) You hear /ôr/ in **fork**. Say **fork**.* (fork) Then read the directions and call students' attention to number 1. Say: *The picture shows a cork in a bottle. Say **cork**.* (cork) *What **vowel + r** sound do you hear in **cork**?* (/ôr/) *What letters stand for that sound?* (or) *Write the letters **or** on the lines to spell the word **cork**.* Repeat this process for the remaining pictures.
Picture Key: 1. cork, 2. horse, 3. barn, 4. horn, 5. artist, 6. stork, 7. shark, 8. alarm, 9. storm

Dictation Direct students' attention to the bottom of the page and say:
Listen to each word I say. Then write the word you hear.   1. arm   2. charm   3. port   4. stork

DAY 2
Listening for R-Controlled Vowels: er, ir, ur

Read aloud the focus statement. Then point to the first example and say: *The letters **e** and **r** together usually have the /ûr/ sound you hear in **fern**. Say /ûr/. (/ûr/) Say **fern**.* (fern) Repeat this process for **ir** and **ur**. Then read the directions and call students' attention to number 1. Say: *The picture shows a herd of cows. Say **herd**.* (herd) *What **vowel + r** sound do you hear in **herd**?* (/ûr/) *What letters have the /ûr/ sound in **herd**?* (er) *Underline the letters **er** in **herd**.* Point out that there is another spelling and meaning for the word **herd**: **heard**, the past tense of **hear**. Repeat this process for the remaining words.

Dictation Direct students' attention to the bottom of the page and say:
Listen to each word I say. Then write the letters that stand for the sounds you hear.
1. skirt   2. stern   3. burn   4. turn

DAY 3
Writing Words with R-Controlled Vowels: ar, or, er, ir, ur

Direct students' attention to the word box at the top of the page. Guide students in reading each word aloud. Then read aloud the directions and call students' attention to number 1. Say: *The first picture shows a shirt. Say **shirt**.* *What **vowel + r** sound do you hear in **shirt**?* (/ûr/) *Find the word **shirt** in the word box and write it on the line.* After students finish writing, ask: *How do you spell **shirt**?* (s-h-i-r-t) Repeat the process for the remaining pictures.
Picture Key: 1. shirt, 2. barn, 3. fern, 4. shark, 5. surf, 6. horn, 7. herd, 8. cork, 9. turtle

Dictation Direct students' attention to the bottom of the page and say:
Listen to this sentence. Then write it on the line: **A herd of cows is in the barn.**

DAY 4
Listening for Words with R-Controlled Vowels: air, are, ear

Read aloud the focus statement. Then point to the first example word as you say: *The letter combination **are** has the /âr/ sound you hear in **square**. Say /âr/. (/âr/) Say **square**.* (square) Repeat this process for the **air** and **ear** spellings of /âr/. Then read the directions and call students' attention to number 1. Say: *The first picture shows a bear. Say **bear**.* (bear) *What letters have the /âr/ sound in **bear**?* (ear) *Underline **ear** in **bear**.* Repeat this process for the remaining words. Point out the pairs of homophones: **hair, hare; pear, pair**.

Dictation Direct students' attention to the bottom of the page and say:
Listen to each word I say. Then write the missing letters to complete the word.
1. wear   2. spare   3. stair (as in what you walk up and down on)   4. rare

DAY 5
Reading Words with R-Controlled Vowels: er, ir, ur, air, are, ear

Read the directions and call students' attention to the picture. Say: *It looks like Marti still needs to find something to wear. Let's read the first incomplete sentence: **What _____ can I _____ today?** Now let's read the words in the gray bar: **horn, shirt, wear**. Which word belongs on the first line?* (shirt) *Write **shirt** on the line. Which word completes the sentence?* (wear) After students finish writing, say: *Now let's read the sentence together: **What shirt can I wear today?*** Repeat this process for the remaining sentences.

Dictation Direct students' attention to the bottom of the page and say:
Listen to this sentence. Then write it on the line: **Will you share your pear with me?**

Listen for It

Focus When a vowel is followed by the letter **r**, the **r** changes the sound of the vowel. The sounds blend together to make a new sound.

| ar
d**ar**t | 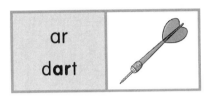 | or
f**or**k |  |

Say the word for the picture.
Write **ar** or **or** to spell the **vowel + r** sound you hear. Then read the word.

1.  c ___ ___ k	2.  h ___ ___ se	3.  b ___ ___ n
4.  h ___ ___ n	5.  ___ ___ tist	6.  st ___ ___ k
7.  sh ___ ___ k	8.  al ___ ___ m	9.  st ___ ___ m

Dictation ••

1. _____ 2. _____ 3. _____ 4. _____

Listen for It

Focus When an **e**, an **i**, or a **u** is followed by an **r**, the vowel sound blends with the **r** to make a new sound. The letter pairs **er**, **ir**, and **ur** usually have the same **vowel + r** sound you hear in **fur**.

fer**n**

dir**t**

pur**se**

Read the word and listen to the **vowel + r** sound.
Underline the letters that have the **vowel + r** sound you hear in **fur**.

1. herd	2. nurse	3. shirt
4. **30** thirty	5. girl	6. surf
7. person	8. circle	9. turtle

Dictation ....

1. ___ ___ ir ___   2. ___ ___ er ___   3. ___ ur ___   4. ___ ur ___

Write It

Word Box

fern	shark	horn
herd	turtle	cork
barn	shirt	surf

Write the word that names the picture.

1.

_____

2.

_____

3.

_____

4.

_____

5.

_____

6.

_____

7.

_____

8.

_____

9.

_____

Dictation •

_____

Name _____

Listen for It

Focus The letter combinations **are**, **air**, and **ear** can all have the vowel + r sound you hear in **care**.

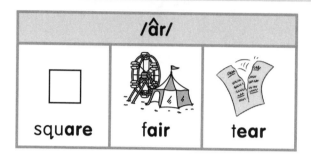

/âr/		
squ**are**	f**air**	t**ear**

Read the word and listen to the **vowel + r** sound.
Underline the letters that have the **vowel + r** sound you hear in **care**.

1.
bear

2.
hair

3.
pear

4.
mare

5.
pair

6.
scare

7.
hare

8.
stare

9.
chair

Dictation ••

1. ___ ear   2. ___ ___ are   3. ___ ___ air   4. ___ are

Read It

Write the two words that best complete the sentence.

| horn | shirt | wear |

1. What _____ can I _____ today?

| tear | person | pair |

2. This _____ of socks has a _____!

| curl | hair | cork |

3. I have no time to _____ my _____.

| term | purse | square |

4. Where is my new _____ _____?

| care | pear | perfect |

5. I don't _____ if I do not look _____!

Dictation •

_____

The Sounds of oo

DAY 1

Listening for the Sounds of oo

Read aloud the focus statement as you point to each example. Have students say each word after you, emphasizing the /o͞o/ or /o͝o/ sound. Then read aloud the directions and call students' attention to the first picture in row 1. Say: *This picture shows a moon. Say* **moon.** *(moon) Do you hear the /o͞o/ or the /o͝o/ vowel sound in* **moon?** *(/o͞o/) Now look at the boot. Does* **boot** *have the same vowel sound as* **moon?** *(yes) Fill in the circle next to the word* **boot.** *The next picture shows a hook. Say* **hook.** *(hook) Does* **hook** *have the same vowel sound as* **moon?** *(no) Do* not *fill in the circle. Repeat this process for the remaining words.*

Dictation Direct students' attention to the bottom of the page and say:
Listen to each word I say. Then write the word on the line. 1. *room* 2. *soon* 3. *good* 4. *look*

DAY 2

Writing Words with the Sounds of oo

Direct students' attention to the word box at the top of the page. Guide students in reading each word aloud. If necessary, have students try saying each word with the /o͞o/ and then the /o͝o/ sound to decide which is correct. Then read aloud the directions and call students' attention to number 1. Say: *The picture shows a hook. Say* **hook.** *(hook) Find the word* **hook** *in the word box and write it on the line.* After students finish writing, ask: *How do you spell* **hook?** *(h-o-o-k) Repeat the process for the remaining pictures.*
Picture Key: 1. hook, 2. cookie, 3. raccoon, 4. spoon, 5. hood, 6. moose, 7. book, 8. football, 9. tooth, 10. wood, 11. broom, 12. boot

Dictation Direct students' attention to the bottom of the page and say:
Listen to each word I say. Then write the word on the line. 1. *pool* 2. *food* 3. *moon* 4. *cook*

DAY 3

Writing Words with the Digraph oo

Read aloud the directions and call students' attention to the word box. Have them read the words aloud. Then have students return to the first word in the word box. Ask: *What does this word say? (cook) Does* **cook** *have the /o͞o/ sound you hear in* **pool** *or the /o͝o/ sound you hear in* **book?** *(/o͝o/ in book) Write the word on the line under* **book.** *Repeat this process for the remaining words.*

Dictation Direct students' attention to the bottom of the page and say:
Listen to this sentence. Then write it on the line: **The cook was in a good mood.**

DAY 4

Reading Words with the Digraph oo

Read aloud the directions and call students' attention to phrase number 1. Say: *Let's read number 1 together:* **the moon on a cool night.** *Do you hear /o͞o/ or /o͝o/ in* **moon?** *(/o͞o/) Underline the word* **moon.** *Do you hear /o͞o/ or /o͝o/ in* **cool?** *(/o͞o/) Underline the word* **cool.** *Now draw a line from the words to the picture that goes with them. Repeat this process for the remaining phrases.*

Dictation Direct students' attention to the bottom of the page and say:
Listen to this sentence. Then write it on the line: **My foot is too big for this boot.**

DAY 5

Reading Words with the Digraph oo

Read the directions and call students' attention to the picture. Say: *This picture shows a girl baking cookies. Let's read the first incomplete sentence:* **I was in the _____ to make _____.** *Now let's read the words in the gray bar:* **noon, cookies, mood.** *Which word belongs on the first line? (mood) Write* **mood** *on the line. Which word should you write on the second line? (cookies) Write* **cookies** *on the line.* After students have finished writing, say: *Now read the sentence with me:* **I was in the mood to make cookies.** *Repeat this process for the remaining sentences.*

Dictation Direct students' attention to the bottom of the page and say:
Listen to this sentence. Then write it on the line: **I stood on a stool to see into the room.**

Listen for It

Focus The vowel pair **oo** is a digraph that can have the vowel sound you hear in **food**. It can also have the vowel sound you hear in **wood**.

Say the first word. Listen to the vowel sound. Then name each picture in the row. Fill in the circle if it has the same vowel sound as the first picture.

1. moon   ○ boot   ○ hook   ○ pool   ○ broom

2. foot   ○ hood   ○ cookie   ○ tooth   ○ book

3. spoon   ○ food   ○ moose   ○ wood   ○ raccoon

Dictation

1. _____   2. _____   3. _____   4. _____

Write It

Word Box

book	cookie	football	hood	hook	broom
moose	spoon	raccoon	tooth	boot	wood

Write the word that names the picture.

1.

_____

2.

_____

3.

_____

4.

_____

5.

_____

6.

_____

7.

_____

8.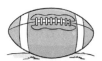

_____

9.

_____

10.

_____

11.

_____

12.

_____

Dictation

1. _____   2. _____   3. _____   4. _____

Name _____

Write It

Day 3 | Week 20

Word Box

cook	brook	cartoon	cool
hoop	mood	moose	stood
foot	wood	shook	spoon

Read each word. Listen to the vowel sound.
Write each word in the box that has the same **oo** sound.

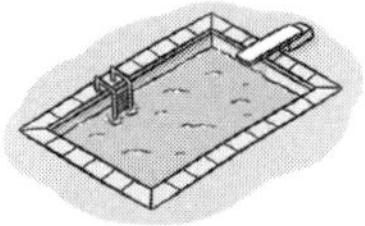

pool

_____

_____

_____

_____

_____

_____

book

_____

_____

_____

_____

_____

_____

Dictation

_____

© Evan-Moor Corp. • EMC 2790 • Daily Phonics Practice   **Skill:** Writing words with **oo** digraphs   **121**

Name _____

Read It

Read the phrase. Underline each word that has the vowel sound in **broom**.
Circle each word that has the vowel sound in **wood**.
Then draw a line to the correct picture.

1. the **moon** on a **cool** night

2. **took** a swim in the **pool**

3. a **loose tooth**

4. a **cookbook** and two **spoons**

5. a **raccoon** that wants **food**

6. a **hood** that **looks good**

Dictation ···

_____

Read It

Write the two words that best complete the sentence.

| noon | cookies | mood |

1. I was in the _____ to make _____.

| good | bookcase | cookbook |

2. I used a _____ _____.

| spoon | wood | stool |

3. I had to mix the batter with a _____ _____.

| noon | snoop | room |

4. My dog came into the _____ to _____.

| stood | cool | drool |

5. She _____ on her back legs and began to _____.

Dictation

_____

Short Vowel Digraphs
ea, ou, ui

DAY 1

Listening for the Short Vowel Sound of ea

Read aloud the focus statement. Then say: *Usually the letters* **e** *and* **a** *together have the* **long e** *sound you hear in words like* **read, team,** *and* **eat.** *Today we are going to read words with* **ea** *that have the* **short e** *sound, /ĕ/, as in* **head.** *Say* **head.** *(head) Then read aloud the directions and call students' attention to number 1. Say: The picture shows a loaf of bread. Say* **bread.** *(bread) Do you hear /ĕ/ in* **bread?** *(yes) Fill in the circle next to* **yes.** *Repeat the process for the remaining words.*

Dictation Direct students' attention to the bottom of the page and say:

Listen to each word I say. Then write the missing letters to complete the word.   1. sweat   2. breath   3. dread

DAY 2

Listening for the Short Vowel Sounds of ou and ui

Read aloud the focus statement. Then point to the first example and say: *We've just learned that the letters* **u** *and* **i** *together can have the* **long u** *sound you hear in* **fruit.** *But the letters* **u** *and* **i** *together can also have the* **short i** *sound, /ĭ/, as in* **build.** *Say* **build.** *(build) Repeat the process for the* **short u** *sound in* **country.** *Then read the directions and call students' attention to number 1. Say: The picture shows a dog getting into trouble. Say* **trouble.** *(trouble) Do you hear /ĭ/ or /ŭ/ in* **trouble?** *(/ŭ/) What letters have the* **short u** *sound? (ou) Underline the* **o** *and* **u** *in* **trouble.** *Repeat this process for the remaining words.*

Dictation Direct students' attention to the bottom of the page and say:

Listen to this sentence. Then write it on the line: **My cousin plays a guitar.**

DAY 3

Writing Words with Short Vowel Digraphs: ea, ou, ui

Direct students' attention to the word box at the top of the page. Guide students in reading each word aloud. Then read the directions and call students' attention to number 1. Say: *The picture shows a double scoop of ice cream. Say* **double.** *(double) Find the word* **double** *in the word box and write it on the line. Repeat this process for the remaining pictures.*

Picture Key: 1. double, 2. bread, 3. quilt, 4. sweater, 5. building, 6. trouble, 7. biscuit, 8. rough, 9. feather, 10. breakfast, 11. guitar, 12. country

Dictation Direct students' attention to the bottom of the page and say:

Listen to this sentence. Then write it on the line: **I had a biscuit for breakfast.**

DAY 4

Writing Words with Short Vowel Digraphs: ea, ou, ui

Read aloud the directions and call students' attention to the word box. Have students read each word aloud. Then say: *Now point to the first word. What does it say?* (building) *What letters have the /ĭ/ sound in* **building?** *(ui) Write the word* **building** *in the box that says* **short i.** *Repeat the process for the remaining words.*

Dictation Direct students' attention to the bottom of the page and say:

Listen to this sentence. Then write it on the line: **Is the quilt heavy enough?**

DAY 5

Reading Words with Short Vowel Digraphs: ea, ou, ui

Read the directions and call students' attention to the picture. Say: *This picture shows a puppy that is in trouble for chewing a sweater. Let's read the first incomplete sentence together:* **My _____ has a cute, _____ puppy.** *Now let's read the words in the gray bar:* **enough, cousin, young.** *Which word belongs on the first line?* (cousin) *Write* **cousin** *on the first line. Which word completes the sentence,* **enough** *or* **young?** *(young) Write* **young** *on the line. After students finish writing, say: Now let's read the sentence together:* **My cousin has a cute, young puppy.** *Repeat this process for the remaining sentences.*

Dictation Direct students' attention to the bottom of the page and say:

Listen to this sentence. Then write it on the line: **We are ready to go into the building.**

Name _____

Listen for It

Focus The vowel digraph **ea** sometimes has the **short e** sound.

| short **e** **hea**d | |

Say the word. Do you hear the **short e** sound?
Fill in the circle next to **yes** or **no**.

1.  ○ yes ○ no
   bread

2.   ○ yes ○ no
   thread

3. ○ yes ○ no
   peach

4.   ○ yes ○ no
   feather

5. ○ yes ○ no
   sweater

6.   ○ yes ○ no
   eagle

7.  ○ yes ○ no
   breakfast

8. ○ yes ○ no
   leaf

9. ○ yes ○ no
   spread

Dictation •

1. ___ ___ ea ___   2. ___ ___ ea ___ ___   3. ___ ___ ea ___

Listen for It

Focus The vowel pair **ui** is a digraph that can have the **short i** sound.
The vowel pair **ou** is a digraph that can have the **short u** sound.

short **i** **bu**ild	short **u** c**ou**ntry

Say the word. Listen for the **short i** or **short u** sound.
Underline the two letters that together have the **short i** or **short u** sound.

1.  trouble	2. quilt	3. rough
4. double	5.  couple	6. 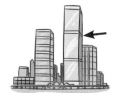 building
7.  guitar	8.  cousins	9.  biscuit

Dictation •

_____

Name _____

Write It

Word Box

quilt	double	biscuit	feather	sweater	building
bread	guitar	rough	country	trouble	breakfast

Write the word that names the picture.

1.

_____

2.

_____

3.

_____

4.

_____

5.

_____

6.

_____

7.

_____

8.

_____

9.

_____

10.

_____

11.

_____

12.

_____

Dictation

_____

© Evan-Moor Corp. • EMC 2790 • Daily Phonics Practice   **Skill:** Writing words with short vowel digraphs   **127**

Write It

Word Box

building	ready	enough	quilt
tough	bread	biscuit	young
guitar	touch	feather	heavy

Read each word. Listen for the **short** vowel sound.
Write the word in the correct box.

short e	short i	short u
head	builder	country

Dictation

_____

Read It

Write the two words that best complete the sentence.

enough	cousin	young

1. My _____ has a cute, _____ puppy.

trouble	building	ready

2. He is always _____ to make _____.

thread	sweater	couple

3. He pulled the _____ out of my _____.

quilt	biscuits	rough

4. He hides his _____ under a _____.

guilty	breath	head

5. Then he looks _____ and hangs his _____.

Dictation •••

_____

Variant Vowel Digraphs
au, aw, al

DAY 1 **Listening for Variant Vowel Sounds: au, aw**

Read aloud the focus statement as you point to each example. Have students say each word after you, emphasizing the /ô/ sound. Then read the directions and call students' attention to number 1. Say: *The picture shows an animal's paw. Say **paw**.* (paw) *What letters in **paw** have the /ô/ sound?* (aw) *Underline the **aw** in **paw**.* Repeat this process for the remaining words.

Dictation   Direct students' attention to the bottom of the page and say:
Listen to each word I say. Then write the letters that stand for the sounds you hear.
1. flaw   2. lawn   3. haunt   4. fault

DAY 2 **Writing Words with Variant Vowel Digraphs: au, aw**

Direct students' attention to the word box at the top of the page. Guide students in reading each word aloud. Then read aloud the directions and call students' attention to number 1. Say: *The first picture shows a crab with its claw circled. Say **claw**.* (claw) *Find the word **claw** in the word box and write it on the line.* After students finish writing, ask: *What letters have the /ô/ sound in **claw**?* (aw) *Circle the letters **aw** in **claw**.* Repeat the process for the remaining pictures.

Picture Key: 1. claw, 2. sauce, 3. paw, 4. haunt, 5. haul, 6. dawn, 7. faucet, 8. straw, 9. yawn

Dictation   Direct students' attention to the bottom of the page and say:
Listen to each word I say. Then write the letters that stand for the sounds you hear.
1. vault   2. launch   3. draw   4. sprawl

DAY 3 **Listening for Variant Vowel Sounds: al**

Read aloud the focus statement as you point to each example. Have students say each word after you, emphasizing the /ô/ sound. Point out that in **ball**, the l is pronounced, but in **talk**, the l is not pronounced. Explain that when the letter l comes before the letter k, the l is often silent. Then read the directions and call students' attention to number 1. Say: *The picture shows two people walking. Say **walk**.* (walk) *Do you hear /ô/ in **walk**?* (yes) *Fill in the circle next to **yes**.* Repeat this process for the remaining words.

Dictation   Direct students' attention to the bottom of the page and say:
Listen to this sentence. Then write it on the line: **Call me if you want to talk.**

DAY 4 **Writing Words with Variant Vowel Digraphs: au, aw, al**

Direct students' attention to the word box at the top of the page. Have students read each word aloud. Then read aloud the directions and call students' attention to number 1. Say: *Let's read the clue together:* **This is when the sun rises.** *Which word from the box tells when the sun rises?* (dawn) *Write **dawn** on the line.* Repeat this process for the remaining clues.

Dictation   Direct students' attention to the bottom of the page and say:
Listen to this sentence. Then write it on the line: **I like to draw with chalk.**

DAY 5 **Reading Words with Variant Vowel Digraphs: au, aw, al**

Read aloud the directions and call students' attention to the picture. Say: *This picture shows a fawn lying under the trees. Let's read the first incomplete sentence together:* **A _____ lies under _____ trees.** *Now let's read the words in the gray bar:* **fawn, fault, tall.** *Which word belongs on the first line?* (fawn) *Write **fawn** on the line. Which word completes the sentence, **fault** or **tall**?* (tall) *Write the word **tall** on the next line.* After students have finished writing, say: *Now let's read the sentence together:* **A fawn lies under tall trees.** Repeat this process for the remaining sentences.

Dictation   Direct students' attention to the bottom of the page and say:
Listen to this sentence. Then write it on the line: **The author will talk about hawks.**

Listen for It

Focus The letter pairs **au** and **aw** are digraphs that can have the vowel sound you hear in **sauce** and in **yawn**.

s**au**ce		y**aw**n	

Say the word and listen for the vowel sound.
Underline the letters that stand for the vowel sound you hear.

1. paw	2. hawk	3.  August
4.  claw	5.  haul	6.  dawn
7.  faucet	8.  author	9. straw

Dictation ••

1. ___ ___aw   2. ___aw___   3. ___au___ ___   4. ___au___ ___

Name _____

Write It

Word Box

claw	haul	faucet
haunt	paw	dawn
straw	yawn	sauce

Write the word that names the picture.
Then circle the letters that stand for the vowel sound you hear.

1.

_____

2.

_____

3.

_____

4.

_____

5.

_____

6.

_____

7.

_____

8.

_____

9.

_____

Dictation

1. ___ au ___ ___   2. ___ au ___ ___   3. ___ ___ ___ aw   4. ___ ___ ___ aw ___

Daily Phonics Practice • EMC 2790 • © Evan-Moor Corp.

Listen for It

Focus When the letter **a** is followed by the letter **l**, the **a** often has the vowel sound you hear in **ball** and in **talk**.

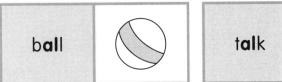

b**all**		t**alk**	

Say the word. Does it have the vowel sound you hear in **ball** and **talk**?
Fill in the circle next to **yes** or **no**.

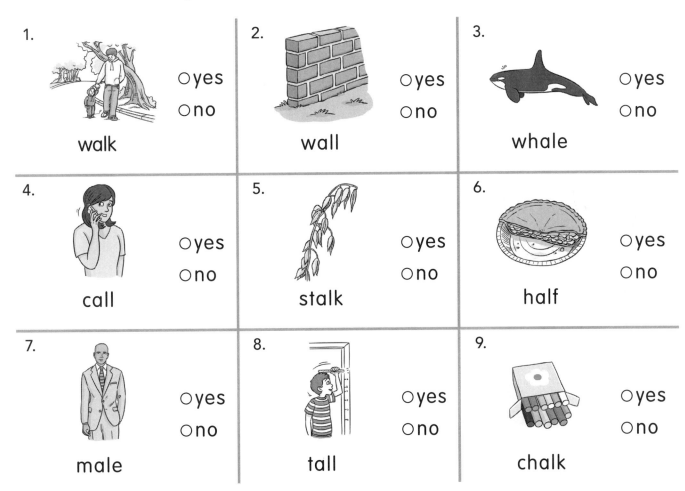

1. ○ yes ○ no
walk

2. ○ yes ○ no
wall

3. ○ yes ○ no
whale

4. ○ yes ○ no
call

5. ○ yes ○ no
stalk

6. ○ yes ○ no
half

7. ○ yes ○ no
male

8. ○ yes ○ no
tall

9. ○ yes ○ no
chalk

Dictation •

_____

Write It

Word Box

chalk	dawn	haul	baseball	faucet
mall	paws	sauce	yawn	August

Write the word that fits the clue.

1. This is when the sun rises.　　　　　 _____

2. You do this when you are sleepy.　 _____

3. A cat has four of these.　　　　　　 _____

4. This is something you can cook.　　 _____

5. This is a month in late summer.　　 _____

6. You can draw with this.　　　　　　 _____

7. A truck can do this.　　　　　　　　 _____

8. This is a place to shop.　　　　　　 _____

9. This is a part of a sink.　　　　　　 _____

10. You can throw this.　　　　　　　　 _____

Dictation ●●●

_____

Read It

Write the two words that best complete the sentence.

| fawn | fault | tall |

1. A _____ lies under _____ trees.

| stalk | crawls | talks |

2. A bug _____ onto a _____ of grass.

| hawk | call | haul |

3. Far away, a _____ begins to _____.

| fall | causes | sauces |

4. The wind _____ the leaves to _____.

| August | author | dawn |

5. It is almost _____ on the last day of _____.

Dictation ....

_____

Diphthongs
ou, ow, oi, oy

DAY 1 Listening for the /ou/ Sound

Read aloud the focus statement as you point to each example. Have students repeat each word after you, emphasizing the /ou/ sound. Then read the directions and call students' attention to number 1. Say: *This person is taking a bow. Say bow.* (bow) *What vowel sound do you hear in bow?* (/ou/) Remind students that the letter pair **ow** can also have the **long o** sound as in the word **bow**, meaning something you tie. Then ask: *What letters in the verb bow have the /ou/ sound?* (ow) *Underline the o and w in bow.* Repeat this process for the remaining words. For number 3, point out that the picture shows a computer mouse. For numbers 4 and 5, point out that the words **flour** and **flower** are homophones, or words that sound alike but have different spellings and meanings.

Dictation Direct students' attention to the bottom of the page and say:

Listen to each word I say. Then write the missing letters to complete the word.
1. loud 2. brown 3. gown 4. sour

DAY 2 Writing Words with Diphthongs: ou, ow

Direct students' attention to the word box at the top of the page. Guide students in reading each word aloud. Then read aloud the directions and call students' attention to number 1. Say: *The picture shows a woman who is frowning.* Demonstrate a frown for students. Then say: *Say frown.* (frown) *Find the word frown in the box. How is it spelled?* (f-r-o-w-n) *Write it on the line under the picture. Then circle the letters that have the /ou/ sound.* Repeat this process for the remaining pictures.
Picture Key: 1. frown, 2. mouse, 3. towel, 4. flower, 5. mouth, 6. crowd, 7. cloud, 8. snout, 9. tower

Dictation Direct students' attention to the bottom of the page and say:

Listen to each word I say. Then write the missing letters to complete the word.
1. crown 2. found 3. shout 4. howl

DAY 3 Listening for the /oi/ Sound

Read aloud the focus statement as you point to each example. Have students repeat each word after you, emphasizing the /oi/ sound. Then read the directions and call students' attention to number 1. Say: *The picture shows a bottle of oil. Say oil.* (oil) *What letters in oil have the /oi/ sound?* (oi) *Underline the o and i in oil.* Repeat this process for the remaining words.

Dictation Direct students' attention to the bottom of the page and say:

Listen to each word I say. Then write the word you hear.   1. soil 2. toy 3. joy 4. point

DAY 4 Writing Words with Diphthongs: oi, oy

Direct students' attention to the word box at the top of the page. Have students read each word aloud. Then read the directions and call students' attention to number 1. Say: *Let's read the clue together: This is a man on a ranch. Which word names someone who is often on a ranch?* (cowboy) *Find the word cowboy in the box and write it on the line.* Repeat this process for the remaining clues.

Dictation Direct students' attention to the bottom of the page and say:

Listen to this sentence. Then write it on the line: The boy put the coins in the bank.

DAY 5 Reading Words with Diphthongs: ou, ow, oi, oy

Read the directions and call students' attention to the picture. Say: *This picture shows a king throwing coins to a crowd of people. Let's read the first incomplete sentence together: The _____ stood _____ in the cold. Now let's read the words in the gray bar: cloud, crowd, outside. Which word belongs on the first line?* (crowd) *Write crowd on the line. Which word completes the sentence, cloud or outside?* (outside) *Write the word outside on the next line.* After students have finished writing, say: *Now let's read the sentence together: The crowd stood outside in the cold.* Repeat this process for the remaining sentences.

Dictation Direct students' attention to the bottom of the page and say:

Listen to this sentence. Then write it on the line: How do I join the scouts?

Listen for It

Focus The letters pairs **ou** and **ow** sometimes have the vowel sound you hear in **couch** and in **frown**.

| couch  | frown |

Read the word and listen to the vowel sound.
Underline the letters that stand for the vowel sound you hear in **how**.

1.
bow

2.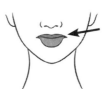
mouth

3.
mouse

4.
flour

5.
flower

6.
towel

7.
south

8.
trout

9.
crowd

Dictation •

1. ___ ou ___   2. ___ ___ ow ___   3. ___ ow ___   4. ___ ou ___

Write It

Word Box

cloud	crowd	frown	flower	mouse
mouth	snout	towel	tower	

Write the word that names the picture.
Then circle the letters that stand for the vowel sound you hear in **how**.

1.

_____

2.

_____

3.

_____

4.

_____

5.

_____

6.

_____

7.

_____

8.

_____

9.

_____

Dictation

1. ____ ____ ow____   2. ____ ou ____ ____   3. ____ ____ ou ____   4. ____ ow ____

Listen for It

Focus The letter pairs **oi** and **oy** have the vowel sound you hear in **coins** and in **boy**. The letter pair **oi** usually comes in the middle of a word. The letter pair **oy** usually comes at the end of a word.

coins		boy	

Read the word and listen to the vowel sound.
Underline the letters that stand for the vowel sound you hear in **toy**.

1. 	2. 	3.
oil	batboy	coin
4. 	5. 	6. 
soil	toys	poison
7. 	8. 	9.
royal	point	coil

Dictation ....

1. _____   2. _____   3. _____   4. _____

Write It

Word Box

royal	boil	cowboy
enjoy	coins	annoy
point	soil	toy

Write the word that fits the clue.

1. This is a man on a ranch. _____

2. This means "to like." _____

3. You use a pot on a stove to do this. _____

4. A plant can grow in this. _____

5. A king and a queen are this. _____

6. This means "to make mad." _____

7. This is a sharp end. _____

8. You pay with these. _____

9. This is something you play with. _____

Dictation

_____

Read It

Write the two words that best complete the sentence.

| cloud | crowd | outside |

1. The _____ stood _____ in the cold.

| tower | towel | royal |

2. They looked up at the king in the _____ _____.

| toys | points | crown |

3. The king wore a _____ with five _____.

| ground | coins | joins |

4. He tossed _____ to the people on the _____.

| scouts | shouts | joy |

5. The crowd gave _____ of _____ when they saw the coins.

Dictation

_____

DAY 1 Listening for Syllables

Read aloud the focus statement. Point to the first example and say: *Listen to this word: flag. Say flag.* (flag) *How many vowel sounds do you hear in flag?* (1—/ă/) *The word flag has one vowel sound, so it has one syllable.* Repeat this process for **window**. Then read the directions and call students' attention to number 1. Say: *The picture shows a glove. Say glove.* (glove) *How many vowel sounds do you hear in glove?* (1) *Write the number 1 in the first box. How many syllables do you hear in glove?* (1) *Write the number 1 in the next box.* If students are having trouble hearing the syllables, have them clap each time they hear a vowel sound. Repeat this process for the remaining words.

Picture Key: 1. glove, 2. menu, 3. tent, 4. tomato, 5. penny, 6. banana

Dictation   Direct students' attention to the bottom of the page and say:

Listen to each word I say. Then write the word on the line. Write the number of syllables in the box.
1. crab   2. sunset   3. napkin

DAY 2 Listening for Syllables

Read aloud the focus statement. Point to the word **cabin** and say: *This word is divided into two syllables. Look at the first syllable. Is it a closed syllable?* (yes) *How do you know it's closed?* (It ends in a consonant. It ends with the letter **b**.) *Will the a have a short or a long sound?* (short) *Now look at the second syllable. Is it a closed syllable?* (yes) *How do you know?* (It ends in a consonant. It ends with the letter **n**.) *Will the i have a short or a long sound?* (short) *Let's read the word together: cabin.* Then read the directions and call attention to number 1. Say: *Look at the first syllable in the word. Is it a closed syllable?* (yes) *Will the u have a short sound?* (yes) *Underline the u. Now point to the second syllable in the word. Is it a closed syllable?* (yes) *Will the i have a short sound?* (yes) *Underline the i. Now let's read the word together: pumpkin.* Repeat this process for the remaining words.

Dictation   Direct students' attention to the bottom of the page and say:

Listen to each word I say. Then write the word on the line.   1. penny   2. robot   3. cabin

DAY 3 Reading Words with Open Syllables

Read aloud the focus statement. Point to the first syllable in the word **robot** and ask: *Is this an open syllable?* (yes) *How do you know?* (It ends in a vowel.) *Will the o have a short or a long sound?* (long) Point to the last syllable and ask: *Is this an open or a closed syllable?* (closed) *What sound will the o have?* (short) Then read the directions and call attention to number 1. Say: *Point to the first syllable in the word.* (hu) *Is it an open or a closed syllable?* (open) *How do you know it's an open syllable?* (It ends in a vowel.) *Will the u have a short or a long sound?* (long) *Underline the u. Let's read the word: human.* Repeat this process for the remaining words, applying the open or closed syllable rule to read each word.

Dictation   Direct students' attention to the bottom of the page and say:

Listen to this sentence. Then write it on the line: **The lady will open the jar.**

DAY 4 Listening for the Accented Syllable

Read aloud the focus statement. Then point to the first example word and say: *Listen to this word: elephant. Say elephant.* (elephant) *Which syllable has an accent mark after it?* (the first one; el) *So which syllable is said with the most stress?* (the first one; el) *Say it with me again: el•e•phant.* Repeat the process with **balloon**. Then read the directions. Call students' attention to number 1 and say: *The words are broken into syllables because we are going to add accent marks to show which syllable is stressed. Let's read the first word together: pencil. Which syllable is stressed?* (the first; pen) *Write an accent mark after the syllable pen in pencil.* Repeat this process for the remaining words.

Dictation   Direct students' attention to the bottom of the page and say:

Listen to this sentence. Then write it on the line: **Will a giraffe eat a hamburger?**

DAY 5 Categorizing Words with Open and Closed Syllables

Read the directions and call students' attention to number 1. Say: *Let's read the word together: penny. The first syllable is underlined. Is the syllable open or closed?* (closed) *How do you know?* (The syllable ends in a consonant—n) *Make a check in the box under closed syllable. Is the underlined syllable stressed or unstressed?* (stressed) *Make a check in the box under stressed.* Repeat this process for the remaining words.

Dictation   Direct students' attention to the bottom of the page and say:

Listen to this sentence. Then write it on the line: **Put the bacon on the napkin.**

Listen for It

Focus A **syllable** is a word part that has only one vowel sound. A word can have more than one syllable.

1 vowel sound = **1** syllable	**2** vowel sounds = **2** syllables
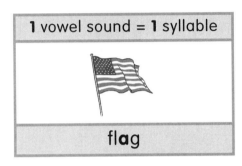	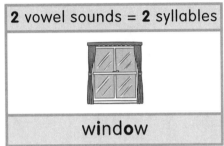
flag	window

Say the word for the picture. Listen for the vowel sound or sounds. Write how many vowel sounds you hear. Then write how many syllables the word has.

	vowel sounds	syllables
1.		
2.		
3.		
4.		
5.		
6.		

Dictation ···

1. _____ ☐   2. _____ ☐   3. _____ ☐

Listen for It

Focus A syllable that ends in a consonant is called a **closed** syllable. The vowel in a closed syllable often has a **short** sound.

cab•in

Look at the syllables in the word. Underline the vowel or vowels that have a **short** sound. Then blend the syllables to read the word.

1. pump•kin

2. pen•ny

3. ro•bot

4. mu•sic

5. pil•low

6. men•u

7. up•set

8. tu•lip

9. lim•it

Dictation •

1. _____ 2. _____ 3. _____

Name _____

Read It

Focus A syllable that ends in a vowel sound is called an **open** syllable. The vowel sound in an open syllable is often a **long** sound.

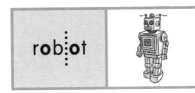

Look at the syllables in the word. Underline the letter or letters that have a **long** sound. Then blend the syllables to read the word.

1. hu•man	2. tu•lip	3. ba•by
4. mi•nus	5. la•dy	6. go•pher
7. ba•con	8. mu•sic	9. o•pen

Dictation ....

_____

Listen for It

Day 4 | Week 24

Focus The syllables in a word can be **stressed** or **unstressed**. A dictionary uses an accent mark (') to show which syllable is **stressed**, or said with the most force.

el•e•phant		bal•loon´	

Read the word. Listen for the syllable that is spoken with the most stress. Write an accent mark after the stressed syllable.

1. 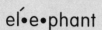 pen • cil	2.  ar • tist	3. car • ton
4. car • toon	5. ham • bur • ger	6. pret • zel
7. brace • let	8. to • ma • to	9. gi • raffe
10. croc • o • dile	11. sal • ad	12. up • set

Dictation ....

_____

Read It

Look at the syllable that is underlined in each word. Read the word out loud.
Then check the correct boxes.

	closed syllable	open syllable	stressed	unstressed
1. p<u>e</u>nny				
2. r<u>o</u>tten				
3. b<u>a</u>con				
4. to<u>ma</u>to				
5. hel<u>lo</u>				
6. nap<u>kin</u>				
7. ro<u>bot</u>				
8. ho<u>tel</u>				

Dictation ···

_____

The Schwa Sound

DAY 1 — **Listening for the Schwa Sound**

Review the definition of a syllable and the difference between a stressed and an unstressed syllable. Then read aloud the focus statement. Point to the first example and say: *This word is **lemon**. Say **lemon**.* (lemon) *How many syllables does **lemon** have?* (2) *Which syllable is stressed?* (the first) *Yes, the first syllable is stressed. The second syllable is unstressed. What sound does the **o** have in the unstressed syllable?* (schwa sound, /uh/) Repeat the process for **little**, **about**, and **compete**. Then read the directions and call students' attention to number 1. Say: *The picture shows a chicken. Say **chicken**.* (chicken) *Which syllable is unstressed in **chicken**?* (second) *Which vowel has the schwa sound in **chicken**?* (e) *Circle the letter **e**.* Repeat this process for the remaining words.

Dictation Direct students' attention to the bottom of the page and say:
Listen to each word I say. Write the missing letters to spell the <u>unstressed</u> syllable.
1. dragon 2. pencil 3. balloon

DAY 2 — **Listening for Final /əl/ and Final /ən/**

Read aloud the focus statement. Then point to the words **level**, **pupil**, and **little** and have students read them with you. Then say: *What sound do you hear at the end of all these words?* (/əl/) Repeat the process for **happen**, **raisin**, and **person**. Then read the directions and call students' attention to number 1. Say: *The picture shows a dragon. Say **dragon**.* (dragon) *What sound do you hear at the end of **dragon**?* (/ən/) *What letters stand for the /ən/ sound in **dragon**?* (on) *Circle the letters **on**.* Repeat this process for the remaining words.

Dictation Direct students' attention to the bottom of the page and say:
*Listen to this sentence. Then write it on the line: **Put the chicken on the table.***

DAY 3 — **Writing Words with /ə/ in the First Syllable**

Read aloud the focus statement. Then read aloud the directions and call students' attention to the word box. Have them read each word aloud. Then say: *Point to the first word. What does it say?* (alone) *What letter has the schwa sound in **alone**?* (a) *Write the word **alone** in the box that says /ə/ **spelled a**.* Repeat the process for the remaining words.

Dictation Direct students' attention to the bottom of the page and say:
*Listen to this sentence. Then write it on the line: **I agree to compete today.***

DAY 4 — **Writing Words with /ə/ in the First, Middle, or Last Syllable**

Read aloud the focus statement. Then read aloud the directions and call students' attention to the word box. Have them read each word aloud. Then say: *Point to the first word. What does it say?* (afraid) *In which syllable do you hear the /ə/ sound in **afraid**?* (first) *Write the word **afraid** in the box that says **first syllable**.* Repeat the process for the remaining words.

Dictation Direct students' attention to the bottom of the page and say:
*Listen to this sentence. Then write it on the line: **A tomato fell out of the wagon.***

DAY 5 — **Reading Words with the Schwa Sound**

Read the directions and call students' attention to the picture. Say: *This picture shows a pond. Let's read the first incomplete sentence together: **The pond _____ a home for many _____**. Now let's read the words in the gray bar: **provides**, **alphabet**, **animals**. Which word belongs on the first line?* (provides) *Write **provides** on the first line. Which word should you write on the second line?* (animals) *Write **animals** on the line.* After students have finished writing, say: *Now let's read the sentence together: **The pond provides a home for many animals**.* Repeat this process for the remaining sentences.

Dictation Direct students' attention to the bottom of the page and say:
*Listen to this sentence. Then write it on the line: **I sat alone at the table today.***

Listen for It

Focus

The vowel in an unstressed syllable often has the **schwa sound**. It is not a long or a short vowel sound. It sounds like /uh/. The schwa sound is written as ə in a dictionary.

lemon	little	about	compete
lem • **ən**	lit • **təl**	**ə** • bout	**cəm** • pete

Say the word. Listen for the unstressed syllable.
Circle the vowel that stands for the **schwa sound**.

1.  chicken	2. nickel	3.  dragon
4.  gerbil	5. shovel	6. balloon
7. tomato	8. pencil	9.  telephone

Dictation •

1. dra_____   2. pen_____   3. _____loon

Listen for It

Focus Many words end with a **schwa + /l/** or a **schwa + /n/** sound.
The **schwa + /l/** sound can be spelled **el**, **il**, or **le**.
The **schwa + /n/** sound can be spelled **en**, **in**, or **on**.

schwa + /l/			schwa + /n/		
lev**el**	pup**il**	litt**le**	happ**en**	rais**in**	pers**on**

Say the word. Listen for the unstressed syllable.
Circle the letters that stand for the **schwa + /l/** or **schwa + /n/** sound.

1. dragon

2. gerbil

3. cabin

4. nickel

5. table

6. kitchen

7. chicken

8. lemon

9. shovel

10. pencil

11. robin

12. circle

Dictation ••

_____

Daily Phonics Practice • EMC 2790 • © Evan-Moor Corp.

Write It

Focus Many words begin with an unstressed syllable. The syllable often has the **schwa sound** spelled with the letter **a** or the letter **o**.

Word Box

alone	compete	parade	balloon
today	amount	collect	provide
agree	conclude	police	afraid

Read each word. Is the **schwa sound** spelled with **a** or **o**?
Write the word in the correct box.

/ə/ spelled **a**	/ə/ spelled **o**
_____	_____
_____	_____
_____	_____
_____	_____
_____	_____
_____	_____

Dictation •

_____

Write It

Focus The schwa sound can be in the **first** syllable, the **middle** syllable, or the **last** syllable of a word.

Word Box

afraid	sudden	wagon	conclude
level	attitude	amount	alphabet
stable	tomato	acrobat	telephone

Read each word. Listen for the **schwa sound**.
Write the word in the box that tells which syllable has the schwa sound.

first syllable	**middle** syllable	**last** syllable
_____	_____	_____
_____	_____	_____
_____	_____	_____
_____	_____	_____

Dictation ···

_____

Read It

Write the two words that best complete the sentence.

provides   alphabet   animals

1. The pond _____ a home for many _____.

aloud   afraid   alone

2. I am not _____ to go to the pond _____.

today   table   level

3. The _____ of the water is high _____.

ribbon   sudden   conclude

4. I _____ there has been a _____ change.

amount   collect   telephone

5. I will _____ a small _____ of water.

Dictation ••

_____

DAY 1

Listening to Words with Silent Letters: k, w, b

Read aloud the focus statement. Then point to the first example and say: *This word is **knife**. Say **knife**.* (knife) *Do you hear /k/ at the beginning of **knife**?* (no) *What sound do you hear?* (/n/) *The **k** in **knife** is silent.* Repeat the process for **write** and **comb**. Then read the directions and call students' attention to number 1. Say: *The arrow is pointing to the wrist. Point to your wrist. Now say **wrist**.* (wrist) *Do you hear the /w/ sound at the beginning of **wrist**?* (no) *What sound do you hear?* (/r/) *The **w** in **wrist** is silent. Cross out the letter **w** to show that it is silent.* Repeat the process with the remaining words.

Dictation   Direct students' attention to the bottom of the page and say:

Listen to each word I say. Then write the word you hear.   1. wrist   2. knob   3. thumb   4. knee

---

DAY 2

Writing Words with Silent Letters: k, w, b

Read aloud the directions and call students' attention to the word box. Have them read each word aloud. Then say: *Point to the first word. What does it say?* (knob) *Which letter is silent in **knob**?* (k) *Write the word **knob** in the box that says **silent k**.* Repeat the process for the remaining words.

Dictation   Direct students' attention to the bottom of the page and say:

Listen to each word I say. Then write the word you hear.   1. knot (as in a knot in a rope)   2. crumb
3. wrap (as in to wrap a gift)   4. kneel

DAY 3

Listening to Words with Silent Letters: h, t, l

Read aloud the focus statement. Then point to the first example and say: *This is the word **ghost**. Say **ghost**.* (ghost) *Do you hear /h/ in **ghost**?* (no) *The **h** in **ghost** is silent.* Repeat the process for the silent **t** in **whistle** and the silent **l** in **calf**. Then read the directions and call students' attention to number 1. Say: *The picture shows three words that rhyme—**cat**, **sat**, and **bat**. Say the word **rhyme**.* (rhyme) *Do you hear the sound of the letter **h** in **rhyme**?* (no) *Cross out the letter **h** to show that it is silent.* Repeat the process with the remaining words. For number 9, point out that the word **wrestle** has two silent letters: **w** and **t**.

Dictation   Direct students' attention to the bottom of the page and say:

*Listen to this sentence. Then write it on the line: **Did the ghost whistle**?*

DAY 4

Writing Words with Silent Letters: h, t, l

Read aloud the directions and call students' attention to the word box. Have them read each word aloud. Then say: *Point to the first word. What does it say?* (listen) *What letter is silent in **listen**?* (t) *Write the word **listen** in the box that says **silent t**.* Repeat the process for the remaining words.

Dictation   Direct students' attention to the bottom of the page and say:

*Listen to this sentence: **I walk to the zoo to see the rhino**. Now write the missing words: **walk, rhino**.*

DAY 5

Reading Words with Silent Letters: k, w, b, h, t, l

Read the directions and call students' attention to the picture. *Say: This picture shows a knight going to a castle. Let's read the first incomplete sentence together: **The _____ rides all the way to the _____**. Now let's read the words in the gray bar: **knight, whistle, castle**. Which word belongs on the first line?* (knight) *Write **knight** on the first line. Which word should you write on the second line?* (castle) *Write **castle** on the line.* After students have finished writing, say: *Now let's read the sentence together: **The knight rides all the way to the castle**.* Repeat this process for the remaining sentences.

Dictation   Direct students' attention to the bottom of the page and say:

*Listen to this sentence: **I use my thumb to write with chalk**. Now write the missing words: **thumb, write, chalk**.*

Listen for It

Focus
Sometimes a consonant is **silent**, or does not have a sound. In words beginning with **kn**, the **k** is usually silent. In words beginning with **wr**, the **w** is usually silent. In words ending with **mb**, the **b** is usually silent.

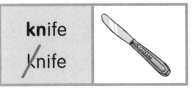 **kn**ife / ~~K~~nife

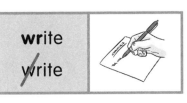 **wr**ite / ~~w~~rite

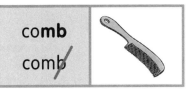 co**mb** / com~~b~~

Say the word. Listen to the letter-sounds.
Then cross out the silent letter and read the word.

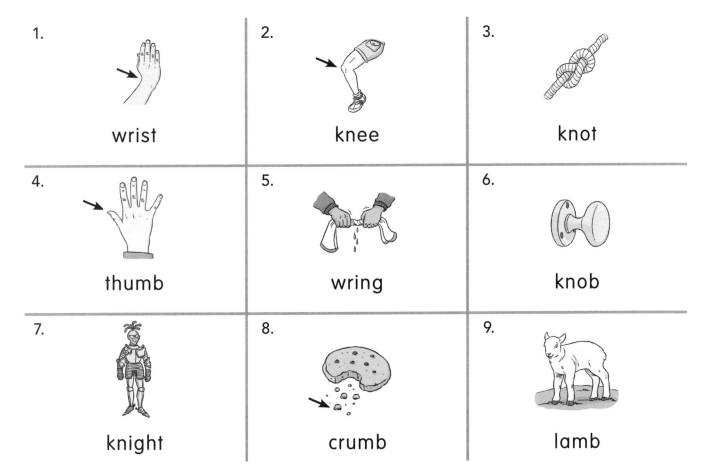

1. wrist

2. knee

3. knot

4. thumb

5. wring

6. knob

7. knight

8. crumb

9. lamb

Dictation •

1. _____   2. _____   3. _____   4. _____

Write It

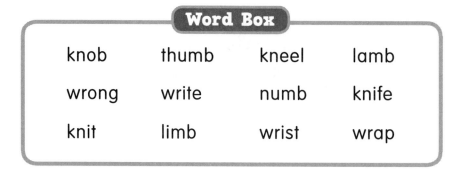

Word Box

knob	thumb	kneel	lamb
wrong	write	numb	knife
knit	limb	wrist	wrap

Read each word. Find the silent letter.
Write the word in the correct box.

silent **k**	silent **w**	silent **b**
_____	_____	_____
_____	_____	_____
_____	_____	_____
_____	_____	_____

Dictation •

1. _____   2. _____   3. _____   4. _____

   Daily Phonics Practice • EMC 2790 • © Evan-Moor Corp.

Listen for It

Focus The consonants **h**, **t**, and **l** are silent in some words.

| ghost
 ~~ghost~~ | | whistle
 ~~whistle~~ | | calf
 ~~calf~~ | |

Say the word. Listen to the letter-sounds.
Then cross out the silent letter or letters and read the word.

1. rhyme	2.  castle	3.  rhino
4.  fasten	5. talk	6. half
7. herb	8.  yolk	9.  wrestle

Dictation •

_____

Write It

Word Box

listen	whistle	walk	rhino
yolk	castle	glisten	herb
ghost	honest	half	chalk

Read each word. Find the silent letter.
Write the word in the correct box.

silent h	silent t	silent l
_____	_____	_____
_____	_____	_____
_____	_____	_____
_____	_____	_____

Dictation

I _____ to the zoo to see the _____.

Read It

Write the two words that best complete the sentence.

| knight | whistle | castle |

1. The _____ rides all the way to the _____.

| knocks | walks | knees |

2. He _____ up to the gate and _____.

| thumb | talk | comb |

3. He must _____ his hair and wait to _____ to the king.

| honest | write | wrong |

4. He will be _____ about what he did _____.

| knows | listen | fastens |

5. The knight _____ the king will _____.

Dictation •

I use my _____ to _____ with _____.

Plural Noun Endings
s, es, ves, ies

DAY 1 **Listening for Words with Plural Endings**

Review the definition of a noun. (a word that names a person, place, or thing) Then read aloud the focus statement. Point to the first example box as you say: *This word is* **book**. *Say* **book**. (book) *Now add an* **s** *to the end and say the new word.* (books) *Do you hear* **/s/** *or* **/z/** *at the end of* **books**? (/s/) Repeat the process for **pens**, emphasizing the **/z/** sound at the end. Then read the directions and call students' attention to number 1. Say: *Does the picture show one hawk or more than one hawk?* (more than one hawk) *Read the words under the picture.* (hawk, hawks) *Which word goes with the picture?* (hawks) *What sound does the* **s** *have at the end of* **hawks**? (/s/) *Fill in the circle next to the word* **hawks**. Repeat this process for the remaining words.

Dictation Direct students' attention to the bottom of the page and say:
Listen to each pair of words I say. Then write the words on the lines. 1. pen pens 2. mask masks

DAY 2 **Writing Words with Plural Endings**

Read aloud the focus statement. Then point to each example word and have students repeat it after you, exaggerating the **schwa + z** (/əz/) sound at the end of the word. Then read the directions and call students' attention to number 1. Ask: *What is the word below the picture?* (dish) *How many dishes are there?* (four) *Because* **dish** *ends in* **sh**, *what is the plural form of* **dish**? (dishes) *Write* **dishes** *on the line. Now let's read the whole phrase:* **four dishes**. Repeat this process for the remaining words.

Dictation Direct students' attention to the bottom of the page and say:
Listen to each word I say. Then add **es** *to write the plural form of the word.*
1. wish (wishes) 2. tax (taxes) 3. inch (inches) 4. kiss (kisses)

DAY 3 **Writing Words with Plural Endings**

Read aloud the focus statement. Point to the example as you say: *The first picture shows a loaf of bread. Say* **loaf**. (loaf) *Since* **loaf** *ends in an* **f**, *to make* **loaf** *plural, you change the* **f** *to* **v** *and add* **es**. *Say* **loaves**. (loaves) Then read the directions and call students' attention to number 1. Ask: *What is the word below the picture?* (leaf) *How many leaves are shown?* (three) *What is the plural form of* **leaf**? (leaves) *Write* **leaves** *on the line. Now let's read the whole phrase:* **three leaves**. Repeat this process for the remaining words. For number 4, point out that the word **knife** ends in **fe**, so the **f** is changed to **v** and only an **s** is added after the silent **e**.

Dictation Direct students' attention to the bottom of the page and say:
Listen to each pair of words I say. Then write the words on the lines.
1. life lives (with a long **i**) 2. shelf shelves

DAY 4 **Writing Words with Plural Endings**

Read aloud the focus statement. Point to the example as you say: *The first picture shows a spy. Say* **spy**. (spy) *Since the word* **spy** *ends with a* **y** *after the consonant* **p**, *to make* **spy** *plural, you change the* **y** *to* **i** *and add* **es**. *Say* **spies**. (spies) *What sound do you hear at the end?* (/z/) Then read the directions and call students' attention to number 1. Ask: *What is the word below the picture?* (fly) *How many flies are there?* (three) *What is the plural form of* **fly**? (flies) *Write* **flies** *on the line. Now let's read the whole phrase:* **three flies**. Repeat this process for the remaining words.

Dictation Direct students' attention to the bottom of the page and say:
Listen to this sentence. Then write it on the line: **Keep the flies away from the berries.**

DAY 5 **Reading Plural Words**

Read the directions and call students' attention to the picture. Say: *This picture shows two ladies who work in a museum. Do they look upset?* (yes) *Why?* (because the locks on the door are broken) *Now let's read the first incomplete sentence together:* **The _____ think that _____ broke into the room.** *Now let's read the words in the gray bar:* **thieves, ladies, berries**. *Which word belongs on the first line?* (ladies) *Write* **ladies** *on the first line. Which word completes the sentence,* **thieves** *or* **berries**? (thieves) *Write* **thieves** *on the line.* After students finish writing, say: *Now let's read the sentence together:* **The ladies think that thieves broke into the room.**

Dictation Direct students' attention to the bottom of the page and say:
Listen to this sentence. Then write it on the line: **Put the dishes on the shelves.**

Name _____

Listen for It

Focus The word **singular** means "one." The word **plural** means "more than one." To make the plural form of most nouns, you add an **s** to the end of the word. The **s** can stand for the /s/ or /z/ sound.

| | book + **s** = books /s/ | | | pen + **s** = pens /z/ | |

Look at the picture and read the words.
Then fill in the circle next to the correct word.

1.
   ○ hawk   ○ hawks

2.
   ○ boot   ○ boots

3.
   ○ grill   ○ grills

4.
   ○ bride   ○ brides

5.
   ○ drum   ○ drums

6.
   ○ spoon   ○ spoons

7.
   ○ nail   ○ nails

8.
   ○ faucet   ○ faucets

9.
   ○ shirt   ○ shirts

Dictation ....

1. _____ _____   2. _____ _____

Write It

Focus When a noun ends with **ch**, **sh**, **ss**, or **x**, an **es** is added to make the noun plural. The **es** ending sounds like /əz/.

 watch**es**  bush**es**  dress**es**  box**es**

Read the word in bold print. Write the plural form of the word on the line. Then read the word you wrote.

1.

dish

four _____

2.
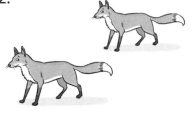
fox

two _____

3.

bench

two _____

4.

glass

three _____

5.

pouch

two _____

6.

brush

five _____

Dictation •

1. _____ 2. _____ 3. _____ 4. _____

Write It

Focus When a noun ends with the letter **f**, the plural form is made by changing the **f** to a **v** and adding **es**.

	v loaf + **es** =	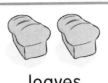 loaves

Read the word in bold print. Write the plural form of the word on the line. Then read the word you wrote.

1.

   leaf

   three _____

2.

   wolf

   three _____

3.

   half

   two _____

4.

   knife

   five _____

5.

   calf

   two _____

6.

   scarf

   two _____

Dictation ....

1. _____ _____   2. _____ _____

Skill: Writing plural nouns

Write It

Focus When a noun ends with a **y** that follows a consonant, the plural form of the noun is made by changing the **y** to **i** and adding **es**. The **s** sounds like /**z**/.

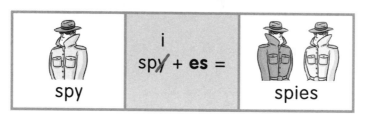

	i sp~~y~~ + **es** =	
spy		spies

Read the word in bold print. Write the plural form of the word on the line. Then read the word you wrote.

1.

fly

three _____

2.

penny

six _____

3.

berry

many _____

4.

candy

four _____

5.

buddy

two _____

6.

mummy

two _____

7.

lady

three _____

8.

baby

two _____

9.

fry

some _____

Dictation •

_____

Name _____

Read It

Day 5 | Week 27

Write the two words that best complete the sentence.

thieves   ladies   berries

1. The _____ think that _____ broke into the room.

boxes   halves   shelves

2. Many _____ are missing from the _____.

flies   dishes   spoons

3. Someone took _____ and _____ made of gold.

pouches   watches   loaves

4. The thieves stole _____ and coins in silk _____.

cases   foxes   mummies

5. The _____ are safe, but why are their _____ open?

Dictation ••

_____

© Evan-Moor Corp. • EMC 2790 • Daily Phonics Practice   **Skill:** Reading plural nouns **165**

Irregular Plural Nouns

DAY 1 — Listening for Irregular Plural Nouns

Read aloud the focus statement. Then point to the first example and have students read the words with you, emphasizing the change from the short **a** to the short **e** sound. (man, men) Ask: *What vowel is changed in **man** to show more than one?* (**a** was changed to **e**) *Men is the plural form of **man**.* Then point to the second example and have students read the words with you. (child, children) Ask: *How is the word **child** changed to show more than one?* (The vowel sound changes from long **i** to short **i**, and the ending **ren** is added.) *Correct, **child** is singular, **children** is plural.* Then read the directions and call students' attention to number 1. Say: *The picture shows one foot. Say the word with me: **foot**. Now find the picture that shows more than one foot. Say the word with me: **feet**. Now draw a line from **foot** to **feet**.* Repeat this process for the remaining words.

Dictation Direct students' attention to the bottom of the page and say:

Listen to each word I say. Write its plural form.   1. *foot* (feet)   2. *tooth* (teeth)   3. *child* (children)

DAY 2 — Writing Irregular Plural Nouns

Read the directions and call students' attention to the word box. Say: *Look at the first word. What does it say?* (feet) *Is the word **feet** singular or plural?* (plural) *Write the word **feet** in the box that says **plural, more than one**.* After students have finished writing, say: *Now find the singular form of **feet** in the word box.* (foot) *Write **foot** in the box that says **singular, one**.* Repeat this process for the remaining words.

Dictation Direct students' attention to the bottom of the page and say:

*Listen to this sentence. Then write it on the line: **The mice ran away from the men.***

DAY 3 — Writing Irregular Plural Nouns

Review the terms **singular** and **plural**. Then read aloud the focus statement. Point to each example and say: *Read the words with me: **fish, fish; jeans, jeans**. We say **fish** when we talk about one fish or more than one fish. We say **jeans** when we talk about one pair or more than one pair of jeans.* Then read the directions and call students' attention to number 1. Say: *Let's read the first phrase: **one moose**. Which word in the phrase is a singular noun?* (moose) *Underline **moose**. Now let's read the second phrase: **a herd of _____**. A **herd** is a group, or more than one. What is the plural form of **moose**?* (moose) *Write the word **moose** on the line. Now let's read the phrase: **a herd of moose**.* Repeat this process for the remaining phrases.

Dictation Direct students' attention to the bottom of the page and say:

Listen and follow my directions: 1. *Write the plural form of **jeans**.*   2. *Write the singular form of **sheep**.*   3. *Write the singular form of **shorts**.*   4. *Write the plural form of **moose**.*

DAY 4 — Writing Irregular Plural Nouns

Direct students' attention to the word box at the top of the page. Have students read each word aloud. Then read aloud the directions and call students' attention to number 1. Say: *Let's read the clue: **These animals can fly**. Which word from the box is the plural form of a type of animal that can fly?* (geese) *Write **geese** on the line.* Repeat this process for the remaining clues.

Dictation Direct students' attention to the bottom of the page and say:

*Listen to this sentence. Then write it on the line: **The women have the same glasses.***

DAY 5 — Reading Irregular Plural Nouns

Read the directions and call students' attention to the picture. Say: *This picture shows two silly sheep who went to a pond. Now let's read the first incomplete sentence together: **Two _____ went to the pond to find some _____**. Now let's read the words in the gray bar: **sheep, sheeps, geese**. Which word belongs on the first line?* (sheep) *Write **sheep** on the first line. Now you know which word to write on the second line.* (geese) After students finish writing, say: *Now let's read the sentence together: **Two sheep went to the pond to find some geese.***

Dictation Direct students' attention to the bottom of the page and say:

*Listen to this sentence. Then write it on the line: **I saw six fish and three geese.***

Listen for It

Focus Some **plural** forms of nouns are very different from their **singular** forms. The vowels might change, or the whole word might change.

 man | men

 child | child**ren**

Say the **singular** word. Draw a line to its **plural** form.

Singular   **Plural**

1. foot •   • people

2. person •   • teeth

3. mouse •   • geese

4. tooth •   • women

5. goose •   • feet

6. woman •   • mice

Dictation ●

1. foot _____ 2. tooth _____ 3. child _____

Skill: Listening for irregular plural nouns

Name _____

Write It

Day 2 | Week 28

Word Box

feet	mouse	geese	foot
child	teeth	woman	children
women	mice	tooth	goose

Read each word.
Write the word in the correct box.

singular **one**	plural **more than one**
_____	_____
_____	_____
_____	_____
_____	_____
_____	_____
_____	_____

Dictation ··

_____

168   **Skill:** Writing irregular plural nouns   Daily Phonics Practice • EMC 2790 • © Evan-Moor Corp.

Write It

Focus | Some nouns have the same **singular** and **plural** forms.

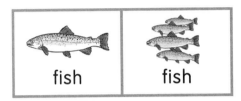

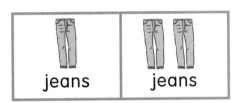

Read the first phrase in each row. Underline the **singular** noun.
Then write the **plural** form of the noun to complete the second phrase.

1.  one moose

    a herd of _____

2. one pair of pants

    two pairs of _____

3. one sheep

    a flock of _____

4. this deer

    those _____

5. my glasses

     two cases of _____

6. one pair of shorts

     two pairs of _____

7. one pair of scissors

    some _____

Dictation •

1. _____   2. _____   3. _____   4. _____

Skill: Writing irregular plural nouns   **169**

Write It

Word Box

glasses	moose	feet	women	mice
scissors	pants	geese	teeth	men

Write the word that fits the clue.

1. These animals can fly. _____

2. These animals are very big. _____

3. You cut with these. _____

4. You chew with these. _____

5. These people are not men. _____

6. You pull these over your legs. _____

7. These help you see. _____

8. You stand on these. _____

9. These people are not women. _____

10. These animals are very small. _____

Dictation ···

_____

Read It

Write the two words that best complete the sentence.

| sheep | sheeps | geese |

1. Two _____ went to the pond to find some _____.

| meese | children | mice |

2. The geese had gone to see two tiny _____ and their young _____.

| feet | glasses | glass |

3. One sheep lost its _____, fell in, and got its _____ wet.

| fish | tooths | teeth |

4. A bunch of _____ bit the sheep with their _____.

| people | pantses | pants |

5. The sheep wished it wore _____ like _____ do!

Dictation ....

_____

DAY 1

Writing Verbs with Inflectional Endings: ed, ing

Read aloud the focus statement. Then point to the first example in the chart and say: *Read this sentence with me: **I paint**. What is the action word?* (paint) *Read the next sentence with me: **I painted last week**. What letters were added to the base word **paint** to put the action in the past?* (ed) *What sound does **ed** have in **painted**?* (/ĭd/) Repeat the process with the sentences in the last column, discussing how the letters **ing** were added to show ongoing action. Then read the directions and call students' attention to the first row. Say: *Let's read the base word together: **pack**. What word is formed by adding **ed** to **pack**?* (packed) *Write **packed** on the line next to **pack**. What sound do the letters **ed** have at the end of **packed**?* (/t/) *Now write the word that is formed by adding **ing** to **pack**.* (packing) Repeat this process for the remaining rows, pointing out the /d/ sound of **ed** in **turned**, **opened**, **rained**, and **listened**; the /t/ sound of **ed** in **talked**; and the /ĭd/ sound in **visited** and **printed**.

Dictation Direct students' attention to the bottom of the page and say:

Listen to each word I say. Then write the word you hear.   1. *walking*   2. *folded*   3. *mixed*   4. *helping*

DAY 2

Writing Verbs with Inflectional Endings: ed, ing

Read aloud the focus statement. Then point to the first example in the chart and say: *Read this sentence with me: **I skate**. What is the action word?* (skate) *What letter does **skate** end with?* (silent e) Point out that **skate** is a CVCe word, which means that the vowel in the middle has a long sound. Then say: *Let's read the next sentence: **I skated last week**. What letter was dropped before **ed** was added to form **skated**?* (silent e) Repeat the process for **skating** in the sentences in the third column. Then point out that **skated** and **skating** still have the long **a** sound even though the silent **e** was dropped. Finally, read the directions and guide students through the activity. Point out the pronunciation differences for the words that end with /t/, /d/, and /ĭd/.

Dictation Direct students' attention to the bottom of the page and say:

Listen to each word I say. Then write the word you hear.   1. *waved*   2. *waving*   3. *biked*   4. *biking*

DAY 3

Writing Verbs with Inflectional Endings: ed, ing

Read aloud the focus statement. Then point to each column of the example chart as students read the sentences with you. Ask: *Which letter is doubled before an ending is added to the word **shop**?* (p) Then read the directions and guide students through the activity, pointing out the pronunciation differences for the words that end with /t/, /d/, and /ĭd/.

Dictation Direct students' attention to the bottom of the page and say:

Listen to each word I say. Then write the word you hear.   1. *slipped*   2. *slipping*   3. *added*   4. *adding*

DAY 4

Writing Verbs with Inflectional Endings: s, es

Read aloud the focus statement. Then read through the examples, using simple sentence frames to model subject-verb agreement. (e.g., *I **paint**; he **paints**. They **skate**; she **skates**.*) Then read the directions and guide students through the activity. After they have finished, have students read aloud each word they wrote.

Dictation Direct students' attention to the bottom of the page and say:

Listen to each sentence I say. Then write it on the line: 1. **The test begins.**   2. **She smiles and relaxes.**

DAY 5

Reading Verbs with Inflectional Endings: ed, ing, s, es

Read the directions and call students' attention to the picture. Say: *This picture shows a boy playing soccer. Let's read the first incomplete sentence together: **Lucas _____ the ball and almost _____ a goal.** Now let's read the words in the gray bar: **scored, scarred, kicked**. Which word belongs on the first line?* (kicked) *Write **kicked** on the first line. Which word completes the sentence: **scored** or **scarred**?* (scored) *Write **scored** on the second line.* After students finish writing, say: *Now let's read the sentence together: **Lucas kicked the ball and almost scored a goal.*** Repeat this process for the remaining sentences.

Dictation Direct students' attention to the bottom of the page and say:

Listen to this sentence. Then write it on the line: **Mom likes to take me shopping.**

Write It

Focus Most **verbs** are action words. When a verb ends with **ed**, it means the action has already happened. When a verb ends with **ing**, it means the action is or was in the process of happening.

action	+ ed	+ ing
I paint.	I paint**ed** last week.	I am paint**ing** now. I was paint**ing** before.

Read the base word. Then write it with each ending.
Read the new words you wrote. Listen for the sound that **ed** has in each word.

action (base word)	+ ed	+ ing
1. pack	_____	_____
2. turn	_____	_____
3. open	_____	_____
4. talk	_____	_____
5. visit	_____	_____
6. rain	_____	_____
7. print	_____	_____
8. listen	_____	_____

Dictation •

1. _____ 2. _____ 3. _____ 4. _____

Write It

Focus   When a verb ends in a **silent e**, you drop the **e** before adding the **ed** or **ing** ending.

action	+ ed	+ ing
I skate.	I skat**ed** last week.	I am skat**ing** now. I was skat**ing** before.

Read the base word. Then follow the rule to add **ed** to the base word.
Follow the rule again to add **ing** to the base word.

action (base word)	+ ed	+ ing
1. save	_____	_____
2. joke	_____	_____
3. like	_____	_____
4. hope	_____	_____
5. trade	_____	_____
6. chase	_____	_____
7. serve	_____	_____
8. decide	_____	_____

Dictation •

1. _____   2. _____   3. _____   4. _____

Write It

Focus When a verb ends with a consonant after a **short vowel** sound, the final consonant is doubled before **ed** or **ing** is added.

action	double the consonant and add **ed**	double the consonant and add **ing**
I shop.	I shop**ped** last week.	I am shop**ping** now. I was shop**ping** before.

Read the base word. Then follow the rule to add **ed** to the base word.
Follow the rule again to add **ing** to the base word.

action (base word)	+ **ed**	+ **ing**
1. zip	_____	_____
2. clap	_____	_____
3. brag	_____	_____
4. chat	_____	_____
5. grin	_____	_____
6. plan	_____	_____
7. shred	_____	_____
8. scrub	_____	_____

Dictation •

1. _____ 2. _____ 3. _____ 4. _____

Name _____

Write It

Sometimes a verb has an **s** or an **es** at the end. This ending shows that only one person or thing is or was doing the action. An **s** is added to verbs that end in a consonant or a **silent e**. An **es** is added to verbs that end in **ch**, **sh**, **ss**, or **x**.

pain**t**	skat**e**	tea**ch**	wa**sh**	to**ss**	fi**x**
pain**ts**	skat**es**	tea**ches**	wa**shes**	to**sses**	fi**xes**

Read the verb. Follow the rule to add **s** or **es**.

1. pass _____	2. mix _____	3. match _____
4. begin _____	5. finish _____	6. relax _____
7. reach _____	8. guess _____	9. brush _____
10. smile _____	11. join _____	12. dress _____

Dictation ....

1. _____ 2. _____

 Daily Phonics Practice • EMC 2790 • © Evan-Moor Corp.

Read It

Write the two words that best complete the sentence.

| scored | scarred | kicked |

1. Lucas _____ the ball and almost _____ a goal.

| rolling | stooped | stopped |

2. The ball was _____ into the net, but Sam _____ it.

| jumping | clipped | clapping |

3. The crowd was _____ and _____ up and down.

| reaches | diving | driving |

4. Sam always _____ the ball by _____ just in time.

| washed | wishes | likes |

5. Lucas _____ Sam and _____ Sam was on his team.

Dictation ●

_____

Contractions

DAY 1 — Reading Contractions That Contain is, are, has, or have

Read the focus statement. Then point to the first example and say: *The words **he is** can be written as the contraction **he's**. What letter was dropped to form the contraction **he's**?* (the **i** in **is**) *What replaced the letter?* (an apostrophe) Repeat this process for **they are**. Then point to the examples for **has** and **have** and say: *When a contraction is formed with **has** or **have**, two letters are dropped. What two letters were dropped from **has** to form the contraction **he's**?* (**h** and **a**) *What two letters were dropped from **have** to form the contraction **they've**?* (**h** and **a**) Point out that the contraction for **he has** looks the same as the contraction for **he is**, but that they mean different things. Then read the directions and call students' attention to number 1. Say: *Let's read the sentence together: **It's cold out.** What two words does **It's** stand for in this sentence?* (It is) *Write **It is** on the lines. Now let's read the new sentence: **It is cold out.*** Repeat this process for the remaining sentences.

Dictation Direct students' attention to the bottom of the page and say:

Listen to the words I say. Write the contraction for those words on the line.
1. we have (we've)   2. they are (they're)   3. she is (she's)   4. he has (he's)

DAY 2 — Reading Contractions That Contain had, would, or will

Read aloud the focus statement. Then point to the first example and say: *The words **she had** can be written as the contraction **she'd**. What letters were dropped to form the contraction **she'd**?* (the **h** and **a** in **had**) Repeat this process for **she would** and **she will**, pointing out that the contraction for **she had** looks the same as the contraction for **she would**, but that they mean different things. Then read the directions and call students' attention to number 1. Say: *Let's read the sentence together: **He'd like to leave soon.** What two words does **He'd** stand for in this sentence?* (He would) *Write **He would** on the lines. Now let's read the new sentence: **He would like to leave soon.*** Repeat this process for the remaining sentences.

Dictation Direct students' attention to the bottom of the page and say:

Listen to the words I say. Write the contraction for those words on the line.
1. I will (I'll)   2. they had (they'd)   3. she would (she'd)   4. you will (you'll)

DAY 3 — Reading Contractions That Contain not

Read aloud the focus statement and guide students through the examples. For **do not/don't**, be sure to point out the vowel-sound change from /ōō/ to /ō/. For **will not/won't**, ask: *What letters were dropped to form the contraction **won't**?* (**ill** in **will**, **o** in **not**) *What replaced these letters?* (**ill** was replaced with **o**; **o** was replaced with an apostrophe) Then read the directions and call students' attention to number 1. Say: *Let's read the phrase together: **she was not.** Now let's read the two contractions: **wasn't, weren't.** Which contraction stands for **was not**?* (wasn't) *Fill in the circle next to **wasn't.*** Repeat this process for the remaining phrases.

Dictation Direct students' attention to the bottom of the page and say:

*Listen to this sentence. Then write it on the line: **You shouldn't go if you aren't well.***

DAY 4 — Writing Contractions

Read the directions and call students' attention to number 1. Say: *Read the two words.* (who is) *Write the contraction for **who is** on the line.* After students finish writing, ask: *What contraction did you write?* (who's) Repeat this process for the remaining words, or have students complete the page independently.

Dictation Direct students' attention to the bottom of the page and say:

*Listen to this sentence. Then write it on the line: **He'll find out if they're here.***

DAY 5 — Reading Contractions

Read the directions and call students' attention to number 1. Say: *Let's read the incomplete sentence together: _____ glad that _____ come to visit us. Now let's read the words in the gray bar: **Weren't, We're, you've.** Which word belongs on the first line?* (We're) *Write **We're** on the first line. Which word completes the sentence, **Weren't** or **you've**?* (you've) After students finish writing, say: *Now let's read the sentence together: **We're glad that you've come to visit us.*** Repeat this process for the remaining sentences.

Dictation Direct students' attention to the bottom of the page and say:

*Listen to this sentence. Then write it on the line: **This isn't where we'll stay.***

Read It

Focus A contraction is a short way of writing two words together. One or more letters in the second word are replaced by an **apostrophe (')**. Many contractions are formed using the verbs **is**, **are**, **has**, and **have**.

is, are	has, have
he ~~is~~ = he**'s**	he ~~has~~ = he**'s**
they ~~are~~ = they**'re**	they ~~have~~ = they**'ve**

Read the sentence. Write the two words that form the **contraction** on the lines. Then read the new sentence.

1. **It's** cold out.   _____ _____ cold out.

2. **They're** here.   _____ _____ here.

3. **What's** your name?   _____ _____ your name?

4. I think **we've** met.   I think _____ _____ met.

5. **You've** grown!   _____ _____ grown!

6. **We're** late.   _____ _____ late.

7. **Here's** a pen.   _____ _____ a pen.

8. **Who's** been here?   _____ _____ been here?

9. **She's** my friend.   _____ _____ my friend.

10. **She's** gone home.   _____ _____ gone home.

11. **They've** come back.   _____ _____ come back.

12. He said **he's** done.   He said _____ _____ done.

Dictation

1. _____   2. _____   3. _____   4. _____

Read It

Focus Many contractions are formed with the words **had**, **would**, and **will**.

| she h~~ad~~ = she**'d** | she w~~oul~~d = she**'d** | she w~~ill~~ = she**'ll** |

Read the sentence. Write the two words that form the **contraction** on the lines. Then read the new sentence.

1. **He'd** like to leave soon.   _____ _____ like to leave soon.

2. **She'd** like to stay.   _____ _____ like to stay.

3. **They'd** arrived last night.   _____ _____ arrived last night.

4. **They'll** stay until tonight.   _____ _____ stay until tonight.

5. **We'd** left by then.   _____ _____ left by then.

6. Do you think **it'll** rain?   Do you think _____ _____ rain?

7. **I'd** bring a hat if I were you.   _____ _____ bring a hat if I were you.

8. **You'll** stay warm and dry.   _____ _____ stay warm and dry.

9. I think **you'd** like my friend.   I think _____ _____ like my friend.

10. **He'll** meet us here at noon.   _____ _____ meet us here at noon.

11. **I'd** hoped to see him before.   _____ _____ hoped to see him before.

12. **He'd** been away last week.   _____ _____ been away last week.

Dictation

1. _____   2. _____   3. _____   4. _____

Read It

Focus   Many contractions are formed with the word **not**.

does n~~o~~t = doesn't	is n~~o~~t = isn't	do n~~o~~t = don't	w~~ill~~ n~~o~~t = won't

Read the phrase. Fill in the circle next to the **contraction** that stands for the bold words.

1. she **was not**   ○ wasn't   ○ weren't

2. they **did not**   ○ don't   ○ didn't

3. he **could not**   ○ couldn't   ○ can't

4. we **will not**   ○ won't   ○ wouldn't

5. it **is not**   ○ doesn't   ○ isn't

6. you **have not**   ○ haven't   ○ hasn't

7. they **are not**   ○ isn't   ○ aren't

8. I **should not**   ○ won't   ○ shouldn't

9. you **were not**   ○ weren't   ○ won't

10. she **has not**   ○ hasn't   ○ wasn't

11. I **cannot**   ○ couldn't   ○ can't

12. he **does not**   ○ doesn't   ○ don't

Dictation ●

_____

Write It

Read the two words. Write their **contraction** on the line.

1. who is _____	2. you are _____	3. he has _____
4. is not _____	5. they would _____	6. I have _____
7. we will _____	8. I had _____	9. does not _____
10. should have _____	11. could not _____	12. they are _____
13. what is _____	14. she has _____	15. there would _____

Dictation •

_____

Read It

Write the two words that best complete the sentence.

> Weren't   We're   you've

1. _____ glad that _____ come to visit us.

> you'd   We'll   We'd

2. _____ hoped that _____ be here by now.

> they've   I'll   you're

3. _____ unpack the car if _____ too tired.

> it's   can't   isn't

4. I _____ believe _____ been a year since we saw you!

> would've   shouldn't   couldn't

5. We _____ gone to see you, but we _____.

Dictation

_____

DAY 1

Reading Words with Prefixes: re, un

Read aloud the focus statement. Then point to the prefix **re** and say: *Many words begin with the prefix **re**. Re means "again." Say **re**.* (re) Then point to the word **replay** and ask: *What word is formed when **re** is added to the base word **play**?* (replay) *Yes, and what does **replay** mean?* (to play again) Then point to the prefix **un** and say: *Some prefixes have more than one meaning.* Guide students through both definitions of **un** and their examples. Then read the directions and call students' attention to number 1. Say: *The first word is **refill**. What prefix does **refill** begin with?* (re) *Circle **re**. What word should you write on the line to complete the definition of **refill**?* (fill) After students finish writing, say: *Now let's read the completed definition together: **to fill again**.* Repeat this process for the remaining words.

Dictation Direct students' attention to the bottom of the page and say:

Listen to each word I say. Then write the word. 1. *untie* 2. *unload* 3. *refill* 4. *restart*

DAY 2

Writing Words with Prefixes: re, un

Read aloud the focus statement and review the meanings of **re** and **un**. Then direct students' attention to the word box. Guide them in reading the words aloud and identifying the prefix and base word in each word. Then read aloud the directions and call students' attention to number 1. Say: *Let's read the definition together: **to heat again**. Which word in the box means "to heat again"?* (reheat) *Write **reheat** on the line.* Repeat this process for the remaining words.

Dictation Direct students' attention to the bottom of the page and say:

Listen to this sentence. Then write it on the line: **They will rebuild the uneven road.**

DAY 3

Reading Words with Prefixes: mis, dis

Read aloud the focus statement. Then point to the prefix **mis** as you say: *Many words begin with the prefix **mis**. Mis means "incorrectly, or badly." Say **mis**.* (mis) Then point to the word **misread** and ask: *When **mis** is added to the base word **read**, what word does it form?* (misread) *Yes, that's right. And what does **misread** mean?* (to read incorrectly) Repeat the process with the prefix **dis**. Then read the directions and call students' attention to number 1. Say: *The first word is **distrust**. What prefix does **distrust** begin with?* (dis) *Circle **dis**. What word should you write on the line to complete the definition of **distrust**?* (trust) After students finish writing, say: *Now let's read the completed definition together: **to not trust**.* Repeat this process for the remaining words.

Dictation Direct students' attention to the bottom of the page and say:

Listen to this sentence. Then write it on the line: **I distrust you because you misbehave.**

DAY 4

Writing Words with Prefixes: mis, dis

Read aloud the focus statement and review the meanings of **mis** and **dis**. Then direct students' attention to the word box. Guide them through the words, helping students identify the prefix and base word of each word. Define any unfamiliar words as necessary. Then read aloud the directions and call students' attention to number 1. Say: *Let's read the definition together: **to treat badly**. Which word in the box means "to treat badly"?* (mistreat) *Write **mistreat** on the line.* Repeat this process for the remaining words.

Dictation Direct students' attention to the bottom of the page and say:

Listen to this sentence. Then write it on the line: **Do not be dishonest or mislead me.**

DAY 5

Reading Words with Prefixes: re, un, mis, dis

Read the directions and call students' attention to number 1. Say: *Let's read the incomplete sentence together:* **James had to _____ the words he _____.** *Now let's read the words in the gray bar:* **rewrite, miscount, misspelled, reheated.** *Which word belongs on the first line?* (rewrite) *Write it on the line. Which word belongs on the second line?* (misspelled) *Write it on the line.* After students have finished writing, say: *Now let's read the complete sentence:* **James had to rewrite the words he misspelled.** Repeat this process for the remaining sentences.

Dictation Direct students' attention to the bottom of the page and say:

Listen to this sentence. Then write it on the line: **You will displease me if you mistreat my cat.**

Read It

Focus A **prefix** is a word part added to the **beginning** of a base word. Each prefix has a meaning. Knowing what a prefix means helps you know what a word means.

re = again
replay = to play **again**

un = not, or the opposite of
unkind = not **kind** **untie** = to do the opposite of **tie**

Read the word in bold print. Circle the **prefix**.
Then write the **base word** on the line to complete the meaning.

1. **refill**   to _____ again

2. **unload**   to do the opposite of _____

3. **unhappy**   not _____

4. **restart**   to _____ again

5. **reread**   to _____ again

6. **unequal**   not _____

7. **unwrap**   to do the opposite of _____

8. **reattach**   to _____ again

9. **unbutton**   to do the opposite of _____

10. **rewrite**   to _____ again

Dictation •••

1. _____   2. _____   3. _____   4. _____

Write It

Focus Each prefix has a meaning. Knowing what a prefix means helps you know what a word means.

re = again	**un** = not, or the opposite of

unlucky	retie	uneven	rewrap	uncover
reheat	unzip	unfair	rebuild	unpack

Write the word from above that matches the meaning.

1. to **heat** again _____

2. not **even** _____

3. to **wrap** again _____

4. to do the opposite of **pack** _____

5. not **fair** _____

6. not **lucky** _____

7. to **tie** again _____

8. to do the opposite of **zip** _____

9. to **build** again _____

10. to do the opposite of **cover** _____

Dictation ....

_____

Read It

Focus Each prefix has a meaning. Knowing what a prefix means helps you know what a word means.

mis = incorrectly, or badly	**dis** = not, or the opposite of
misread = to **read** incorrectly	**dislike** = to not **like** **displease** = to do the opposite of **please**

Read the word in bold print. Circle the **prefix**.
Then write the **base word** on the line to complete the meaning.

1. **distrust**   to not _____

2. **disagree**   to not _____

3. **misspell**   to _____ incorrectly

4. **disconnect**   to do the opposite of _____

5. **mistreat**   to _____ badly

6. **mislead**   to _____ incorrectly

7. **disappear**   to do the opposite of _____

8. **disrespect**   to not _____

9. **misspeak**   to _____ incorrectly

10. **misbehave**   to _____ badly

Dictation •

_____

Write It

Focus Each prefix has a meaning. Knowing what a prefix means helps you know what a word means.

mis = incorrectly, or badly	**dis** = the opposite of

disagree	mistreat	dishonest	disconnect	misunderstand
miscount	misjudge	disrespect	disappear	mislead

Write the word from above that matches the meaning.

1. to treat **badly** _____

2. to **count** incorrectly _____

3. the opposite of **respect** _____

4. to do the opposite of **agree** _____

5. to **judge** incorrectly _____

6. to do the opposite of **connect** _____

7. to **understand** incorrectly _____

8. to be the opposite of **honest** _____

9. to do the opposite of **appear** _____

10. to **lead** incorrectly _____

Dictation •

_____

Read It

Write the two words that best complete the sentence.

| rewrite | miscount | misspelled | reheated |

1. James had to _____ the words he _____ .

| unhappy | untie | unequal | unfair |

2. It is _____ to give _____ amounts of candy.

| restart | disconnect | disagree | unload |

3. I _____ that we need to _____ the race.

| misbehave | misjudged | reattach | displeased |

4. Bela _____ how long it would take to _____ the tire.

| dishonest | unlucky | uncover | distrust |

5. I will _____ the truth even if you are _____ .

| misspeak | refill | misunderstand | unkind |

6. Did Rafael _____ , or did I _____ him?

Dictation

_____

DAY 1

Reading Words with Suffixes: ful, less, ly

Read aloud the focus statement. Then point to the suffix **ful** and say: *Many words end with the suffix* **ful**. *Ful means "full of." Say* **ful**. (ful) Then point to the word **helpful** and ask: *What word is formed when* **ful** *is added to the base word* **help**? (helpful) *Yes, and what does* **helpful** *mean?* (full of help) Then point to the suffix **less** and say: *The suffix* **less** *means the opposite of* **ful**. Guide students through the definition and example. Repeat the process for **ly**. Then read the directions and call students' attention to number 1. Say: *The first word is* **hopeful**. *What suffix does* **hopeful** *end with?* (ful) *Circle* **ful**. *What word should you write on the line to complete the definition of* **hopeful**? (hope) After students finish writing, say: *Now let's read the completed definition together:* **full of hope**. Repeat this process for the remaining words.

Dictation   Direct students' attention to the bottom of the page and say:

Listen to each word I say. Then write the word on the line.   1. *useful*   2. *fearless*   3. *sadly*

DAY 2

Writing Words with Suffixes: ful, less, ly

Read aloud the focus statement and review the meanings of **ful**, **less**, and **ly**. Then direct students' attention to the word box. Guide them in reading the words aloud and identifying the suffix and base word of each word. Then read aloud the directions and call students' attention to number 1. Say: *Let's read the definition together:* **without fear**. *Which word in the box means "without fear"?* (fearless) *Write* **fearless** *on the line.* Repeat this process for the remaining words.

Dictation   Direct students' attention to the bottom of the page and say:

Listen to each word I say. Then write the word on the line.   1. *painful*   2. *harmless*   3. *badly*

DAY 3

Reading Words with Suffixes: er, or, ness

Read aloud the focus statement. Then point to the suffix **er** and say: *Many words end with the suffix* **er**. *Er means "a person who." Say* /ər/. (/ər/) Then point to the suffix **or** and say: *This suffix also has the* /ər/ *sound and means "a person who." Point to the word* **teacher** *and ask: When* **er** *is added to the base word* **teach**, *what word does it form?* (teacher) *Yes, and what does* **teacher** *mean?* (a person who teaches) Repeat the process for the suffix **or**. Then guide students through the definitions and examples for **ness**. Finally, read the directions and call students' attention to number 1. Say: *The first word is* **leader**. *What suffix does* **leader** *end with?* (er) *Circle* **er**. *What word should you write on the line to complete the definition of* **leader**? (leads) After students finish writing, say: *Now let's read the completed definition together:* **a person who leads**. Repeat this process for the remaining words.

Dictation   Direct students' attention to the bottom of the page and say:

Listen to this sentence. Then write it on the line: **A painter can't paint in darkness.**

DAY 4

Writing Words with Suffixes: er, or, ness

Read aloud the focus statement and review the meanings of **er**, **or**, and **ness**. Then direct students' attention to the word box. Guide them through the words, helping students identify the suffix and base word of each word. Then read aloud the directions and call students' attention to number 1. Say: *Let's read the definition together:* **the act of being fair**. *Which word in the box means "the act of being fair"?* (fairness) *Write* **fairness** *on the line.* Repeat this process for the remaining words.

Dictation   Direct students' attention to the bottom of the page and say:

Listen to this sentence. Then write it on the line: **A good leader shows fairness.**

DAY 5

Reading Words with Suffixes: ful, less, ly, er, or, ness

Read the directions and call students' attention to number 1. Say: *Let's read the incomplete sentence together:* **I wrote a story about a _____ _____ in a boat.** *Now let's read the words in the gray bar:* **sailor, visitor, painful, careless**. *Which word makes the most sense on the first line?* (careless) *Which word makes sense on the second line?* (sailor) *Write the words on the lines.* After students have finished writing, say: *Now let's read the complete sentence:* **I wrote a story about a careless sailor in a boat.** Repeat for the remaining sentences.

Dictation   Direct students' attention to the bottom of the page and say:

Listen to this sentence. Then write it on the line: **I was careless and got a painful cut.**

Read It

Focus A **suffix** is a word part added to the **end** of a base word. Each suffix has a meaning. Knowing what a suffix means helps you know what a word means.

ful = full of	**less** = without	**ly** = in a certain way
helpful = full of **help**	**helpless** = without **help**	**nicely** = in a **nice** way

Read the word in bold print. Circle the **suffix**.
Then write the **base word** on the line to complete the meaning.

1. **hopeful**   full of _____

2. **painless**   without _____

3. **fearful**   full of _____

4. **tightly**   in a _____ way

5. **clearly**   in a _____ way

6. **powerless**   without _____

7. **graceful**   full of _____

8. **colorful**   full of _____

9. **harmless**   without _____

10. **fairly**   in a _____ way

11. **useless**   without _____

12. **loudly**   in a _____ way

Dictation

1. _____   2. _____   3. _____

Write It

Focus Each suffix has a meaning. Knowing what a suffix means helps you know what a word means.

| **ful** = full of | **less** = without | **ly** = in a certain way |

| softly | colorless | nicely | loosely | painful | helpless |
| harmful | powerful | weakly | careless | fearless | careful |

Write the word from above that matches the meaning.

1. without **fear** _____

2. full of **care** _____

3. in a **nice** way _____

4. full of **power** _____

5. without **color** _____

6. in a **weak** way _____

7. in a **loose** way _____

8. full of **pain** _____

9. in a **soft** way _____

10. without **help** _____

11. without **care** _____

12. full of **harm** _____

Dictation •

1. _____   2. _____   3. _____

Read It

Focus Each suffix has a meaning. Knowing what a suffix means helps you know what a word means.

er and **or** = a person who
teacher = a person who **teaches**   **actor** = a person who **acts**

ness = the act or state of
kindness = the act of being **kind**   **softness** = the state of being **soft**

Read the word in bold print. Circle the **suffix**.
Then write the **base word** on the line to complete the meaning.

1. **leader**   a person who _____

2. **visitor**   a person who _____

3. **sadness**   the state of being _____

4. **inventor**   a person who _____

5. **fairness**   the act of being _____

6. **farmer**   a person who _____

7. **painter**   a person who _____

8. **darkness**   the state of being _____

9. **weakness**   the state of being _____

10. **player**   a person who _____

Dictation •

_____

Write It

Focus Each suffix has a meaning. Knowing what a suffix means helps you know what a word means.

er and **or** = a person who	**ness** = the act or state of

sadness	visitor	fairness	darkness	actor
kindness	farmer	teacher	inventor	writer

Write the word from above that matches the meaning.

1. the act of being **fair**   _____

2. a person who **farms**   _____

3. a person who **teaches**   _____

4. the state of being **dark**   _____

5. a person who **acts**   _____

6. the state of being **sad**   _____

7. a person who **writes**   _____

8. a person who **invents**   _____

9. the act of being **kind**   _____

10. a person who **visits**   _____

Dictation •

_____

Read It

Write the two words that best complete the sentence.

> sailor   visitor   painful   careless

1. I wrote a story about a _____ _____ in a boat.

> quickly   darkly   quickness   darkness

2. The sailor sailed into _____ and _____ got lost.

> harmful   fearful   loudly   loudness

3. The sailor felt _____ and yelled _____ for help.

> powerless   tightly   tightness   powerful

4. He held on _____ as a _____ wind blew.

> kindly   kindness   helpless   helpful

5. Finally, another boater rescued the _____ sailor and showed him _____ .

> kindness   teacher   hopeless   hopeful

6. I am _____ that my _____ will like my story.

Dictation

_____

_____

Answer Key

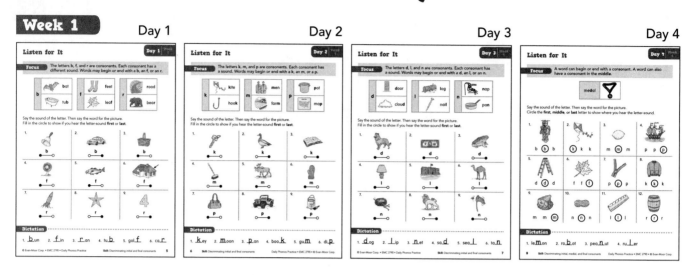

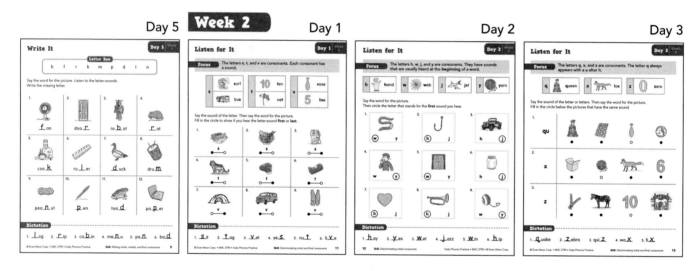

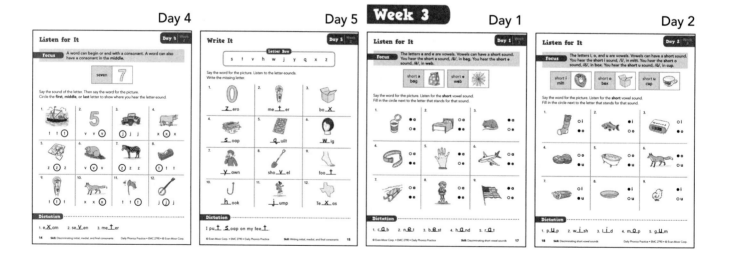

Daily Phonics • EMC 2790 • © Evan-Moor Corp.

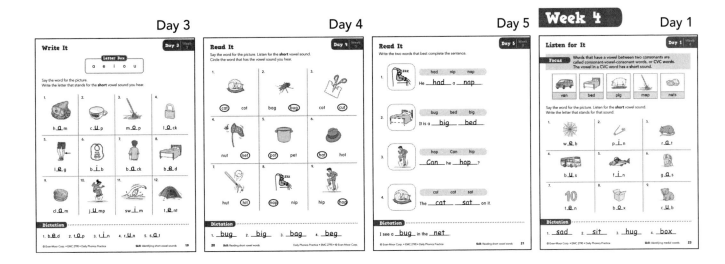

Write It · Day 3
Letter Box
a e i o u
Say the word for the picture.
Write the letter that stands for the **short** vowel sound you hear.
1. h_a_m 2. c_u_p 3. m_o_p 4. l_o_ck
5. l_e_g 6. b_i_b 7. b_a_ck 8. b_e_d
9. cl_a_m 10. j_u_mp 11. sw_i_m 12. t_e_nt
Dictation
1. b_ed_ 2. t_op_ 3. l_i_n 4. r_u_n 5. s_a_t
© Evan-Moor Corp. • EMC 2790 • Daily Phonics Practice   Skill: Identifying short vowel sounds   19

Read It · Day 4
Say the word for the picture. Listen for the **short** vowel sound.
Circle the word that has the vowel sound you hear.
1. (cat) cot 2. bag (bug) 3. cot (cut)
4. nut (net) 5. (pot) pet 6. (hat) hot
7. hut (hit) 8. (nap) nip 9. hip (hop)
Dictation
1. _bug_ 2. _big_ 3. _bag_ 4. _beg_
20   Skill: Reading short vowel words   Daily Phonics Practice • EMC 2790 • © Evan-Moor Corp.

Read It · Day 5
Write the two words that best complete the sentence.
1. had nip nap   He _had_ a _nap_.
2. bug bed big   It is a _big_ _bed_.
3. hop Can hip   _Can_ he _hop_?
4. cot cat sat   The _cat_ _sat_ on it.
Dictation
I see a _bug_ in the _net_.
© Evan-Moor Corp. • EMC 2790 • Daily Phonics Practice   Skill: Reading short vowel words   21

Listen for It · Day 1
Focus Words that have a vowel between two consonants are called consonant-vowel-consonant words, or CVC words. The vowel in a CVC word has a **short** sound.
van bed pig mop nuts
Say the word for the picture. Listen for the **short** vowel sound.
Write the letter that stands for that sound.
1. w_e_b 2. p_i_n 3. r_a_t
4. b_u_s 5. t_i_n 6. g_a_s
7. t_e_n 8. b_o_x 9. c_u_b
Dictation
1. _sad_ 2. _sit_ 3. _hug_ 4. _box_
© Evan-Moor Corp. • EMC 2790 • Daily Phonics Practice   Skill: Identifying medial vowels   23

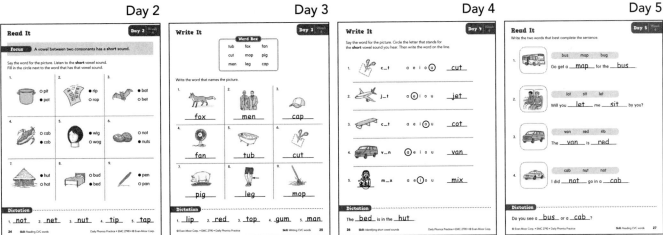

Read It · Day 2
Focus A vowel between two consonants has a **short** sound.
Say the word for the picture. Listen to the **short** vowel sound.
Fill in the circle next to the word that has that vowel sound.
1. ○ pit ● pot 2. ● rip ○ rap 3. ● bat ○ bet
4. ○ cab ● cob 5. ● wig ○ wag 6. ○ not ● nuts
7. ● hut ○ hat 8. ○ bud ● bed 9. ● pen ○ pan
Dictation
1. _not_ 2. _net_ 3. _nut_ 4. _tip_ 5. _tap_
24   Skill: Reading CVC words   Daily Phonics Practice • EMC 2790 • © Evan-Moor Corp.

Write It · Day 3
Word Box
tub fox fan
cut mop pig
men leg cap
Write the word that names the picture.
1. _fox_ 2. _men_ 3. _cap_
4. _fan_ 5. _tub_ 6. _cut_
7. _pig_ 8. _leg_ 9. _mop_
Dictation
1. _lip_ 2. _red_ 3. _top_ 4. _gum_ 5. _man_
© Evan-Moor Corp. • EMC 2790 • Daily Phonics Practice   Skill: Writing CVC words   25

Write It · Day 4
Say the word for the picture. Circle the letter that stands for the **short** vowel sound you hear. Then write the word on the line.
1. c_t a e i o (u) _cut_
2. j_t a (e) i o u _jet_
3. c_t a e i (o) u _cot_
4. v_n (a) e i o u _van_
5. m_x a e (i) o u _mix_
Dictation
The _bed_ is in the _hut_.
26   Skill: Identifying short vowel sounds   Daily Phonics Practice • EMC 2790 • © Evan-Moor Corp.

Read It · Day 5
Write the two words that best complete the sentence.
1. bus map bug   Go get a _map_ for the _bus_.
2. lot sit let   Will you _let_ me _sit_ by you?
3. van red rib   The _van_ is _red_.
4. cab nut not   I did _not_ go in a _cab_.
Dictation
Do you see a _bus_ or a _cab_?
© Evan-Moor Corp. • EMC 2790 • Daily Phonics Practice   Skill: Reading CVC words   27

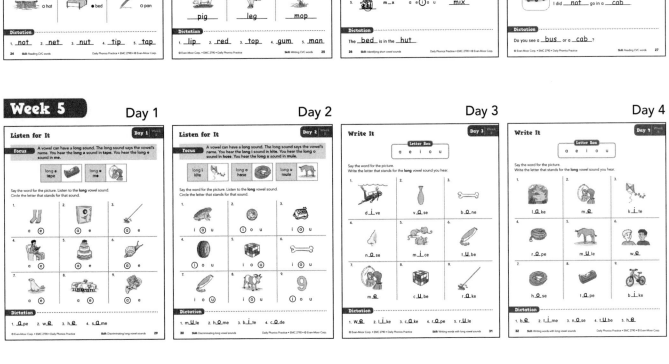

Listen for It · Day 1
Focus A vowel can have a **long** sound. The long sound says the vowel's name. You hear the **long a** sound in **tape**. You hear the **long e** sound in **me**.
long a tape   long e me
Say the word for the picture. Listen to the **long** vowel sound.
Circle the letter that stands for that sound.
1. a (e) 2. (a) e 3. (a) e
4. a (e) 5. (a) e 6. a (e)
7. a (e) 8. a (e) 9. (a) e
Dictation
1. _pe_ 2. w_e_ 3. h_e_ 4. s_a_me
© Evan-Moor Corp. • EMC 2790 • Daily Phonics Practice   Skill: Discriminating long vowel sounds   29

Listen for It · Day 2
Focus A vowel can have a **long** sound. The long sound says the vowel's name. You hear the **long i** sound in **kite**. You hear the **long o** sound in **hose**. You hear the **long u** sound in **mule**.
long i kite   long o hose   long u mule
Say the word for the picture. Listen to the **long** vowel sound.
Circle the letter that stands for that sound.
1. i (o) u 2. (i) o u 3. i (o) u
4. (i) o u 5. i o (u) 6. i (o) u
7. i o (u) 8. (i) o u 9. (i) o u
Dictation
1. m_u_le 2. h_o_me 3. b_i_te 4. c_o_se
30   Skill: Discriminating long vowel sounds   Daily Phonics Practice • EMC 2790 • © Evan-Moor Corp.

Write It · Day 3
Letter Box
a e i o u
Say the word for the picture.
Write the letter that stands for the **long** vowel sound you hear.
1. d_i_ve 2. v_a_se 3. b_o_ne
4. n_o_se 5. m_i_ce 6. t_u_be
7. m_e_ 8. c_u_be 9. r_a_ke
Dictation
1. w_e_ 2. l_i_ke 3. c_a_ke 4. r_o_pe 5. r_u_le
© Evan-Moor Corp. • EMC 2790 • Daily Phonics Practice   Skill: Writing words with long vowel sounds   31

Write It · Day 4
Letter Box
a e i o u
Say the word for the picture.
Write the letter that stands for the **long** vowel sound you hear.
1. l_a_ke 2. m_e_ 3. k_i_te
4. r_o_pe 5. m_u_le 6. w_e_
7. h_o_se 8. t_a_pe 9. b_i_ke
Dictation
1. b_e_ 2. t_i_me 3. n_o_se 4. t_u_be 5. r_a_ke
32   Skill: Writing words with long vowel sounds   Daily Phonics Practice • EMC 2790 • © Evan-Moor Corp.

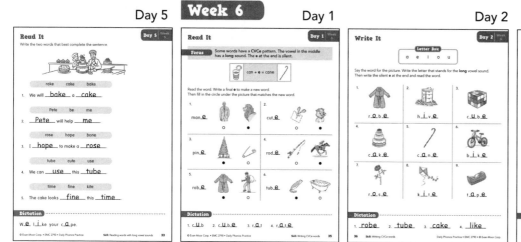
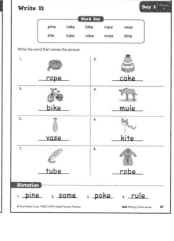

Day 5 — **Week 6** — **Day 1** — **Day 2** — **Day 3**

Read It — Day 5 Week 6
Write the two words that best complete the sentence.

rake   cake   bake
1. We will __bake__ a __cake__

Pete   be   me
2. __Pete__ will help __me__

rose   hope   bone
3. I __hope__ to make a __rose__

tube   cute   use
4. We can __use__ this __tube__

time   fine   kite
5. The cake looks __fine__ this __time__

Dictation
W e   l i k e   your c a pe.

Read It — Day 1 Week 6
Focus Some words have a CVCe pattern. The vowel in the middle has a **long** sound. The **e** at the end is silent.

can + e = cane

Read the word. Write a final **e** to make a new word.
Then fill in the circle under the picture that matches the new word.

1. man_e_
2. cut_e_
3. pin_e_
4. rod_e_
5. rob_e_
6. tub_e_

Dictation
1. c u b   2. c u b e   3. r a t   4. r a te

Write It — Day 2 Week 6
Letter Box
a e i o u

Say the word for the picture. Write the letter that stands for the **long** vowel sound. Then write the silent **e** at the end and read the word.

1. r o b e
2. h i v e
3. c u b e
4. c a k e
5. c a n e
6. b i k e
7. r o s e
8. k i t e
9. t a p e

Dictation
1. robe   2. tube   3. cake   4. like

Write It — Day 3 Week 6
Word Box
pine   cake   bike   rope   vase
kite   tube   robe   mule   dine

Write the word that names the picture.
1. rope   2. cake
3. bike   4. mule
5. vase   6. kite
7. tube   8. robe

Dictation
1. pine   2. same   3. poke   4. rule

Day 4 — **Day 5** — **Week 7** — **Day 1** — **Day 2**

Read It — Day 4 Week 6
Look at the picture. Read the words. Circle the word that names the picture.
1. tame / (time)
2. (pane) / pine
3. mile / (mule)
4. (cake) / cape
5. (fire) / fine
6. like / (lake)
7. (tire) / tore

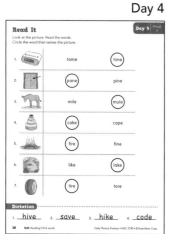

Dictation
1. hive   2. save   3. hike   4. code

Read It — Day 5 Week 6
Write the two words that best complete the sentence.

mule   ride   mule
1. You can __ride__ a __mule__

like   hike   lake
2. Pete and I can __hike__ to the __lake__

hole   hope   cute
3. There is a __cute__ fox in the __hole__

pine   dine   tube
4. You can __dine__ under a __pine__

tide   time   take
5. We can __take__ our __time__

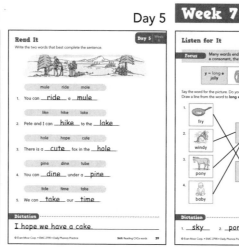

Dictation
I hope we have a cake.

Listen for It — Day 1 Week 7
Focus Many words end with the letter y. When the y comes after a consonant, the y can have a **long e** or a **long i** sound.

y = long e   jelly
y = long i   cry

Say the word for the picture. Do you hear **long e** or **long i**? Draw a line from the word to **long e** or **long i**.

1. fry
2. windy
3. pony
4. baby
long e
long i
5. fly
6. candy
7. sky
8. mummy

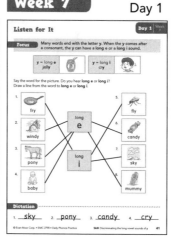

Dictation
1. sky   2. pony   3. candy   4. cry

Listen for It — Day 2 Week 7
Focus A syllable is a word part that has one vowel sound. A y usually has the **long i** sound at the end of a word that has one syllable. A y usually has the **long e** sound at the end of a word that has two syllables.

y = long i   cry   1 syllable
y = long e   baby   2 syllables

Say the word. How many syllables do you hear? Fill in the circle next to that number. Then fill in the circle next to i or e to show what sound the y has.

	syllables	y
penny	○1 ●2	○i ●e
lady	○1 ●2	○i ●e
sunny	○1 ●2	●i ●e
fry	●1 ○2	●i ○e
sky	●1 ○i	●i ●e
fly	○1 ○2	●i ○e

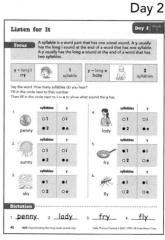

Dictation
1. penny   2. lady   3. fry   4. fly

Day 3 — **Day 4** — **Day 5** — **Week 8** — **Day 1**

Write It — Day 3 Week 7
Word Box
rusty   mummy   dry   penny   spy
cry   my   windy   sly   lazy

Read each word. Do you hear **long e** or **long i**? Write the word in the correct box.

y = long e	y = long i
rusty	dry
mummy	spy
penny	cry
windy	my
lazy	sly

Dictation
She is a sly lady.

Read It — Day 4 Week 7
Look at the picture. Read the words. Circle the word that names the picture.
1. lazy / (baby) / lady
2. dry / (spy) / cry
3. (windy) / try / foggy
4. penny / sly / (fry)
5. candy / (sandy) / silly
6. (muddy) / mummy / my
7. fly / rusty / (jelly)

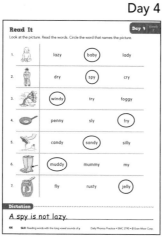

Dictation
A spy is not lazy.

Read It — Day 5 Week 7
Write the two words that best complete the sentence.

me   pony   my
1. I like to ride __my__ __pony__

sky   sandy   sunny
2. We ride when the __sky__ is __sunny__

cry   dusty   dry
3. My face gets __dusty__ and __dry__

muddy   funny   fry
4. At the lake, I __try__ not to get __muddy__

happy   lazy   windy
5. I am __happy__ that my pony is not __lazy__

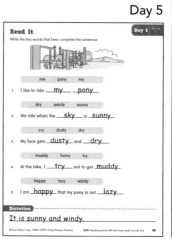

Dictation
It is sunny and windy.

Listen for It — Day 1 Week 8
Focus The letter c can have the **hard** sound of /k/ or the **soft** sound of /s/. The c has the /k/ sound when it is followed by an a, an o, or a u. The c has the /s/ sound when it is followed by an e or an i.

c = /k/ sound: cat   cot   cup
c = /s/ sound: face   city

Say the word and listen for the sound of c. Fill in the circle below **hard c** or **soft c**.

1. cone — hard c ● / soft c ○
2. mice — hard c ○ / soft c ●
3. pencil — hard c ○ / soft c ●
4. cart — hard c ● / soft c ○
5. rice — hard c ○ / soft c ●
6. vacuum — hard c ● / soft c ○

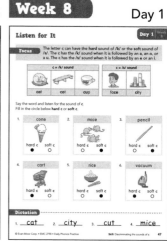

Dictation
1. cat   2. city   3. cut   4. mice

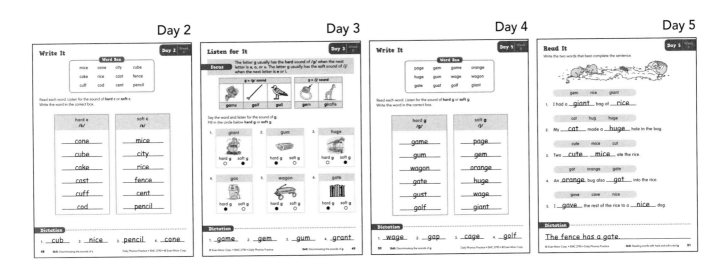

Week 9

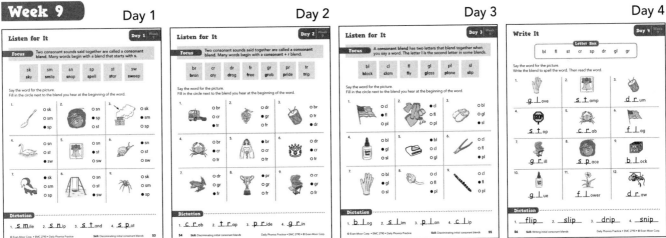

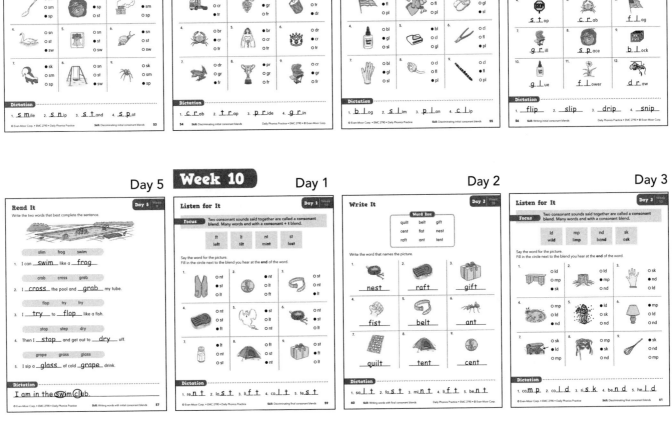

Day 4

Write It

Word Box

cold	stamp	jump
gold	lamp	hand
desk	mask	sand

Write the word that names the picture.

1. mask
2. jump
3. desk
4. stamp
5. gold
6. sand
7. lamp
8. cold
9. hand

Dictation
1. hu_sk_ 2. wi_nd_ 3. bu_mp_ 4. mo_ld_ 5. da_mp_

62 **Skill** Writing words with final consonant blends · Daily Phonics Practice · EMC 2790 · © Evan-Moor Corp.

Day 5

Read It
Day 5 Week 10

Write the two words that best complete the sentence.

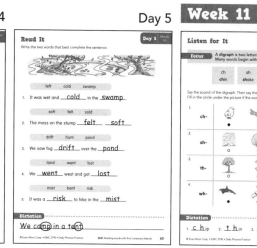

| left | cold | swamp |

1. It was wet and _cold_ in the _swamp_.

| soft | felt | sold |

2. The moss on the stump _felt_ _soft_.

| drift | hunt | pond |

3. We saw fog _drift_ over the _pond_.

| land | went | lost |

4. We _went_ west and got _lost_.

| mist | bent | risk |

5. It was a _risk_ to hike in the _mist_.

Dictation
We camp in a tent.

© Evan-Moor Corp. · EMC 2790 · Daily Phonics Practice   **Skill** Reading words with final consonant blends   63

Week 11

Day 1

Listen for It
Day 1 Week 11

Focus A digraph is two letters together that have one new sound. Many words begin with a consonant + h digraph.

ch	sh	th	wh
chin	shake	thin	why

Say the sound of the digraph. Then say the word for each picture in the row.
Fill in the circle under the picture if the word begins with that digraph.

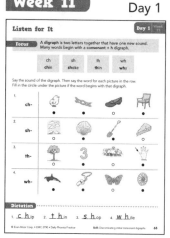

1. ch-
2. sh-
3. th-
4. wh-

Dictation
1. _ch_ip 2. _th_in 3. _sh_op 4. _wh_ile

© Evan-Moor Corp. · EMC 2790 · Daily Phonics Practice   **Skill** Discriminating initial consonant digraphs   65

Day 2

Write It
Day 2 Week 11

Focus A digraph is two letters together that have one new sound.

Letter Box

| ch | sh | th | wh |

Say the word for the picture.
Write the digraph to complete the word. Then read the word.

1. _th_ree
2. _ch_in
3. _ch_ild
4. _sh_ip
5. _wh_ale
6. _sh_ell
7. _th_umb
8. _wh_eel
9. _ch_est
10. _sh_eep

Dictation
1. _ch_amp 2. _th_ick 3. _wh_en 4. _sh_ape

66 **Skill** Writing initial consonant digraphs · Daily Phonics Practice · EMC 2790 · © Evan-Moor Corp.

Day 3

Listen for It
Day 3 Week 11

Focus Many words end with a consonant + h digraph.

ch	sh	th
much	rush	with

Say the word for the picture.
Write the digraph to complete the word. Then read the word.

1. ca_sh_
2. lun_ch_
3. pa_th_
4. ma_th_
5. bru_sh_
6. ba_th_
7. in_ch_
8. ben_ch_
9. fi_sh_

Dictation
1. pu_sh_ 2. nor_th_ 3. su_ch_ 4. cra_sh_

© Evan-Moor Corp. · EMC 2790 · Daily Phonics Practice   **Skill** Discriminating final consonant digraphs   67

Day 4

Listen for It
Day 4 Week 11

Focus A digraph may begin or end a word.

Say the word for the picture.
Fill in the circle to show if you hear the digraph **first** or **last**.

1. sh
2. th
3. wh
4. ch
5. sh
6. th
7. wh
8. th
9. sh

Dictation
1. fla_sh_ 2. mun_ch_ 3. pa_th_ 4. mo_th_

68 **Skill** Discriminating initial and final consonant digraphs · Daily Phonics Practice · EMC 2790 · © Evan-Moor Corp.

Day 5

Read It
Day 5 Week 11

Write the two words that best complete the sentence.

| lunch | fresh | with |

1. Have a _fresh_ taco for _lunch_.

| which | both | fish |

2. We _both_ put _fish_ in our taco.

| crunch | shells | crash |

3. I like to _crunch_ on the _shells_.

| ships | chips | three |

4. May I have _three_ of your _chips_?

| dish | white | when |

5. I will take your _dish_ _when_ you are done.

Dictation
A whale is not a fish.

© Evan-Moor Corp. · EMC 2790 · Daily Phonics Practice   **Skill** Reading words with initial and final consonant digraphs   69

Week 12

Day 1

Listen for It
Day 1 Week 12

Focus The letter pairs ck and ng are digraphs. The ck digraph has the /k/ sound. The ng digraph has the sound you hear at the end of ring. Many words end with these digraphs.

ck	ng
lock	swing

Say the word for the picture.
Fill in the circle next to the digraph you hear at the **end** of the word.

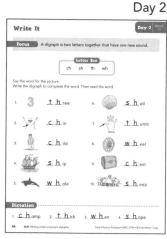

1. ○ ck ● ng
2. ● ck ○ ng
3. ● ck ○ ng
4. ● ck ○ ng
5. ○ ck ● ng
6. ● ck ○ ng
7. ○ ck ● ng
8. ○ ck ● ng
9. ● ck ○ ng

Dictation
1. tri_ck_ 2. bri_ng_ 3. lu_ck_ 4. si_ng_

© Evan-Moor Corp. · EMC 2790 · Daily Phonics Practice   **Skill** Discriminating final consonant digraphs   71

Day 2

Write It
Day 2 Week 12

Letter Box

| ck | ng |

Say the word for the picture and listen to the **final** sound.
Write the digraph that stands for that sound. Then read the word.

1. lo_ck_
2. swi_ng_
3. tru_ck_
4. ki_ck_
5. bri_ck_
6. ha_ng_
7. wi_ng_
8. si_ng_
9. clo_ck_

Dictation
1. ru_ng_ 2. si_ck_ 3. alo_ng_ 4. sha_ck_

72 **Skill** Writing words with final consonant digraphs · Daily Phonics Practice · EMC 2790 · © Evan-Moor Corp.

Day 3

Listen for It
Day 3 Week 12

Focus A digraph is two letters together that have one sound. The digraphs ph and gh usually have the /f/ sound.

ph	gh
phone	laugh

Say the word. Listen to the letter-sounds.
Underline the letters that together have the /f/ sound.

1. dolphin
2. cough
3. graph
4. photo
5. elephant
6. rough
7. trophy
8. alphabet
9. gopher

Aa Bb Cc Dd Ee Ff Gg Hh Ii Jj Kk Ll

Dictation
1. _ph_one 2. tou_gh_ 3. gra_ph_ 4. cou_gh_

© Evan-Moor Corp. · EMC 2790 · Daily Phonics Practice   **Skill** Discriminating consonant digraphs   73

Day 4

Write It
Day 4 Week 12

Word Box

dolphin	elephant	gopher
phone	photo	graph
rough	trophy	laugh

Write the word that names the picture.
Underline the letters that together have the /f/ sound.

1. rough
2. trophy
3. graph
4. photo
5. laugh
6. phone
7. dolphin
8. gopher
9. elephant

Dictation
1. _trophy_ 2. _photo_ 3. _rough_

74 **Skill** Writing words with consonant digraphs · Daily Phonics Practice · EMC 2790 · © Evan-Moor Corp.

Day 5

Read It
Day 5 Week 12

Write the two words that best complete the sentence.

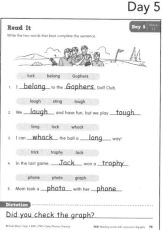

| luck | belong | Gophers |

1. I _belong_ to the _Gophers_ Golf Club.

| laugh | sting | tough |

2. We _laugh_ and have fun, but we play _tough_.

| long | lock | whack |

3. I can _whack_ the ball a _long_ way!

| trick | trophy | Jack |

4. In the last game, _Jack_ won a _trophy_.

| phone | photo | graph |

5. Mom took a _photo_ with her _phone_.

Dictation
Did you check the graph?

© Evan-Moor Corp. · EMC 2790 · Daily Phonics Practice   **Skill** Reading words with consonant digraphs   75

Week 13

Day 1
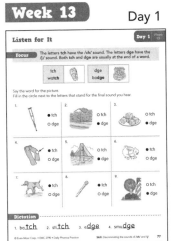

Day 2
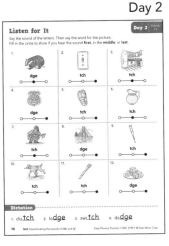

Day 3
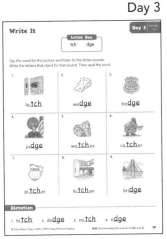

Day 4

Day 5

Week 14

Day 1

Day 2
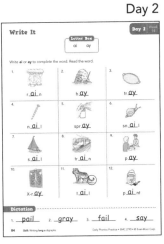

Day 3

Day 4
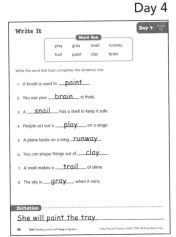

Day 5
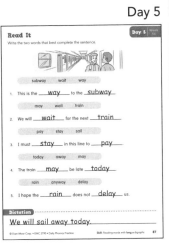

Week 15

Day 1

Day 2

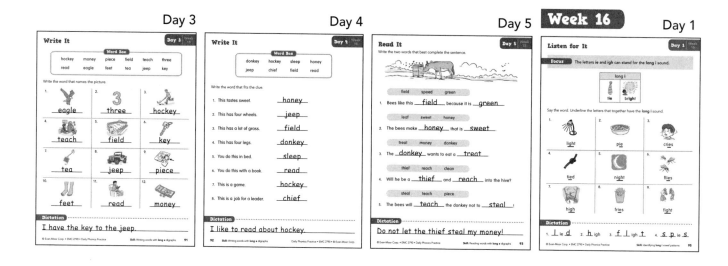

Day 3

Write It — Day 3 Week 16

Word Box: hockey · money · piece · field · teach · three · read · eagle · feet · tea · jeep · key

Write the word that names the picture.
1. eagle 2. three 3. hockey
4. teach 5. field 6. key
7. tea 8. jeep 9. piece
10. feet 11. read 12. money

Dictation
I have the key to the jeep.

© Evan-Moor Corp. • EMC 2790 • Daily Phonics Practice — Skill: Writing words with long e digraphs — 91

Day 4

Write It — Day 4 Week 16

Word Box: donkey · hockey · sleep · honey · jeep · chief · field · read

Write the word that fits the clue.
1. This tastes sweet. — honey
2. This has four wheels. — jeep
3. This has a lot of grass. — field
4. This has four legs. — donkey
5. You do this in bed. — sleep
6. You do this with a book. — read
7. This is a game. — hockey
8. This is a job for a leader. — chief

Dictation
I like to read about hockey.

92 — Skill: Writing words with long e digraphs — Daily Phonics Practice • EMC 2790 • © Evan-Moor Corp.

Day 5

Read It — Day 5 Week 16

Write the two words that best complete the sentence.
1. field · speed · green — Bees like this __field__ because it is __green__.
2. leaf · sweet · honey — The bees make __honey__ that is __sweet__.
3. treat · money · donkey — The __donkey__ wants to eat a __treat__.
4. thief · reach · clean — Will he be a __thief__ and __reach__ into the hive?
5. steal · teach · piece — The bees will __teach__ the donkey not to __steal__!

Dictation
Do not let the thief steal my money!

© Evan-Moor Corp. • EMC 2790 • Daily Phonics Practice — Skill: Reading words with long e digraphs — 93

Week 16

Day 1

Listen for It — Day 1 Week 16

Focus: The letters ie and igh can stand for the long i sound.

long i — tie · bright

Say the word. Underline the letters that together have the long i sound.
1. light 2. pie 3. cries
4. tied 5. night 6. flies
7. high 8. fries 9. fight

Dictation
1. l_ie_d 2. h_igh_ 3. fl_igh_t 4. sp_ie_s

© Evan-Moor Corp. • EMC 2790 • Daily Phonics Practice — Skill: Identifying long i vowel patterns — 95

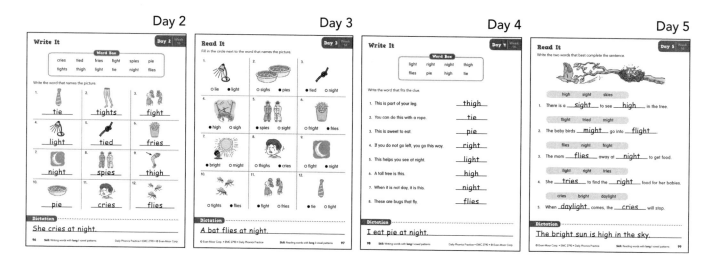

Day 2

Write It — Day 2 Week 16

Word Box: cries · tied · fries · fight · spies · pie · tights · thigh · light · tie · night · flies

Write the word that names the picture.
1. tie 2. tights 3. fight
4. light 5. tied 6. fries
7. night 8. spies 9. thigh
10. pie 11. cries 12. flies

Dictation
She cries at night.

96 — Skill: Writing words with long i vowel patterns — Daily Phonics Practice • EMC 2790 • © Evan-Moor Corp.

Day 3

Read It — Day 3 Week 16

Fill in the circle next to the word that names the picture.
1. ○ lie ● light
2. ○ sighs ● pies
3. ● tied ○ night
4. ● high ○ sigh
5. ● spies ○ sight
6. ○ fright ● fries
7. ● bright ○ might
8. ○ thighs ● cries
9. ○ fight ● night
10. ○ tights ● flies
11. ● fight ○ fries
12. ○ tie ○ light

Dictation
A bat flies at night.

© Evan-Moor Corp. • EMC 2790 • Daily Phonics Practice — Skill: Reading words with long i vowel patterns — 97

Day 4

Write It — Day 4 Week 16

Word Box: light · right · high · thigh · flies · pie · high · tie

Write the word that fits the clue.
1. This is part of your leg. — thigh
2. You can do this with a rope. — tie
3. This is sweet to eat. — pie
4. If you do not go left, you go this way. — right
5. This helps you see at night. — light
6. A tall tree is this. — high
7. When it is not day, it is this. — night
8. These are bugs that fly. — flies

Dictation
I eat pie at night.

98 — Skill: Writing words with long i vowel patterns — Daily Phonics Practice • EMC 2790 • © Evan-Moor Corp.

Day 5

Read It — Day 5 Week 16

Write the two words that best complete the sentence.
1. high · sight · skies — There is a __sight__ to see __high__ in the tree.
2. flight · tried · might — The baby birds __might__ go into __flight__.
3. flies · night · fright — The mom __flies__ away at __night__ to get food.
4. fight · right · tries — She __tries__ to find the __right__ food for her babies.
5. cries · bright · daylight — When __daylight__ comes, the __cries__ will stop.

Dictation
The bright sun is high in the sky.

© Evan-Moor Corp. • EMC 2790 • Daily Phonics Practice — Skill: Reading words with long i vowel patterns — 99

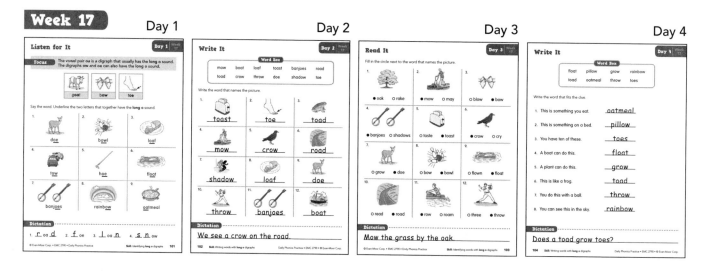

Week 17

Day 1

Listen for It — Day 1 Week 17

Focus: The vowel pair oa is a digraph that usually has the long o sound. The digraphs ow and oe can also have the long o sound.

goat · bow · toe

Say the word. Underline the two letters that together have the long o sound.
1. doe 2. bowl 3. loaf
4. tow 5. hoe 6. float
7. banjoes 8. rainbow 9. oatmeal

Dictation
1. r_oa_d 2. f_oe_ 3. l_oa_n 4. s_n_ow

© Evan-Moor Corp. • EMC 2790 • Daily Phonics Practice — Skill: Identifying long o digraphs — 101

Day 2

Write It — Day 2 Week 17

Word Box: mow · boat · loaf · toast · banjoes · road · toad · crow · throw · doe · shadow · toe

Write the word that names the picture.
1. toast 2. toe 3. toad
4. mow 5. crow 6. road
7. shadow 8. loaf 9. doe
10. throw 11. banjoes 12. boat

Dictation
We see a crow on the road.

102 — Skill: Writing words with long o digraphs — Daily Phonics Practice • EMC 2790 • © Evan-Moor Corp.

Day 3

Read It — Day 3 Week 17

Fill in the circle next to the word that names the picture.
1. ● oak ○ rake
2. ● mow ○ may
3. ○ blow ● bow
4. ● banjoes ○ shadows
5. ○ taste ● toast
6. ● crow ○ cry
7. ○ grow ● doe
8. ○ bow ● bowl
9. ○ flown ● float
10. ○ read ● road
11. ○ row ● roam
12. ○ three ● throw

Dictation
Mow the grass by the oak.

© Evan-Moor Corp. • EMC 2790 • Daily Phonics Practice — Skill: Identifying words with long o digraphs — 103

Day 4

Write It — Day 4 Week 17

Word Box: float · pillow · grow · rainbow · toad · oatmeal · throw · toes

Write the word that fits the clue.
1. This is something you eat. — oatmeal
2. This is something on a bed. — pillow
3. You have ten of these. — toes
4. A boat can do this. — float
5. A plant can do this. — grow
6. This is like a frog. — toad
7. You do this with a ball. — throw
8. You can see this in the sky. — rainbow

Dictation
Does a toad grow toes?

104 — Skill: Writing words with long o digraphs — Daily Phonics Practice • EMC 2790 • © Evan-Moor Corp.

Read It — Day 5

Write the two words that best complete the sentence.

1. The _goat_ wants the hay to _grow_.
   (grow coat goat)
2. The _rainbow_ is _low_ in the sky.
   (rainbow low toast)
3. The _road_ _goes_ over the hill.
   (bowl goes road)
4. The wind _blows_ the _oak_ tree.
   (blows glows oak)
5. Some _crows_ have _flown_ away.
   (flown crows doe)

Dictation
Show me that coat.

Listen for It — Day 1

Focus The letter pairs ue, ew, and ui are digraphs that usually have the long u sound.
(clue grew fruit)

Say the word. Underline the two letters that together have the long u sound.

1. blew   2. glue   3. chew
4. juice   5. suit   6. news
7. fuel   8. flew   9. rescue

Dictation
1. t r ue   2. ch ew   3. st ew   4. d ue l

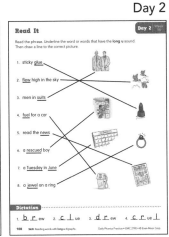

Read It — Day 2

Read the phrase. Underline the word or words that have the long u sound. Then draw a line to the correct picture.

1. sticky glue
2. flew high in the sky
3. men in suits
4. fuel for a car
5. read the news
6. a rescued boy
7. a Tuesday in June
8. a jewel on a ring

Dictation
1. br ew   2. cl ue   3. dr ew   4. cr ue l

Write It — Day 3

Word Box
suit chew clue flew fuel glue
fruit news rescue screw threw Tuesday

Write the word that names the picture.

1. Tuesday   2. threw   3. glue
4. fuel   5. news   6. fruit
7. rescue   8. suit   9. clue
10. chew   11. flew   12. screw

Dictation
We flew to his rescue.

Write It — Day 4

Word Box
fuel chew jewel glue
Tuesday suits blew stew

Write the word that fits the clue.

1. You use your teeth to do this. _chew_
2. This sticks to things. _glue_
3. This can be red, blue, or green. _jewel_
4. This is something you eat. _stew_
5. A car needs this. _fuel_
6. This is a day of the week. _Tuesday_
7. This can be something the wind did. _blew_
8. Men wear these. _suits_

Dictation
We made stew on Tuesday.

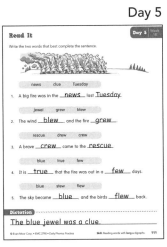

Read It — Day 5

Write the two words that best complete the sentence.

1. A big fire was in the _news_ last _Tuesday_.
   (news clue Tuesday)
2. The wind _blew_ and the fire _grew_.
   (jewel grew blew)
3. A brave _crew_ came to the _rescue_.
   (rescue drew crew)
4. It is _true_ that the fire was out in a _few_ days.
   (blue true few)
5. The sky became _blue_ and the birds _flew_ back.
   (blue stew flew)

Dictation
The blue jewel was a clue.

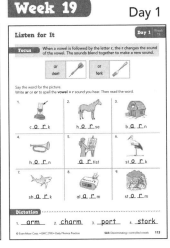

Listen for It — Day 1

Focus When a vowel is followed by the letter r, the r changes the sound of the vowel. The sounds blend together to make a new sound.
(ar dart or fork)

Say the word for the picture. Write ar or or to spell the vowel + r sound you hear. Then read the word.

1. c or k   2. h or se   3. b ar n
4. h or n   5. a r tist   6. st or k
7. sh ar k   8. al ar m   9. st or k

Dictation
1. arm   2. charm   3. port   4. stork

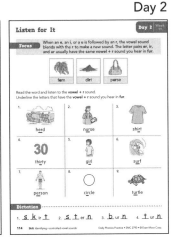

Listen for It — Day 2

Focus When an e, an i, or a u is followed by an r, the vowel sound blends with the r to make a new sound. The letter pairs er, ir, and ur usually have the same vowel + r sound you hear in fur.
(fern dirt purse)

Read the word and listen to the vowel + r sound. Underline the letters that have the vowel + r sound you hear in fur.

1. herd   2. nurse   3. shirt
4. 30 thirty   5. girl   6. surf
7. person   8. circle   9. turtle

Dictation
1. sk ir t   2. st er n   3. b ur n   4. t ur n

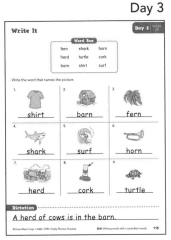

Write It — Day 3

Word Box
fern shark horn
herd turtle cork
barn shirt surf

Write the word that names the picture.

1. shirt   2. barn   3. fern
4. shark   5. surf   6. horn
7. herd   8. cork   9. turtle

Dictation
A herd of cows is in the barn.

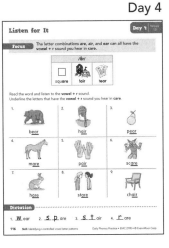

Listen for It — Day 4

Focus The letter combinations are, air, and ear can all have the vowel + r sound you hear in care.
/air/
(square fair tear)

Read the word and listen to the vowel + r sound. Underline the letters that have the vowel + r sound you hear in care.

1. bear   2. hair   3. pear
4. mare   5. pair   6. scare
7. hare   8. stare   9. chair

Dictation
1. w ear   2. sp are   3. st air   4. r are

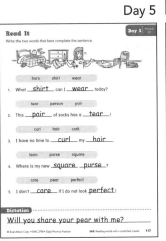

Read It — Day 5

Write the two words that best complete the sentence.

1. What _shirt_ can I _wear_ today?
   (horn shirt wear)
2. This _pair_ of socks has a _tear_!
   (tear person pair)
3. I have no time to _curl_ my _hair_.
   (curl hair cork)
4. Where is my new _square_ _purse_?
   (term purse square)
5. I don't _care_ if I do not look _perfect_!
   (care pear perfect)

Dictation
Will you share your pear with me?

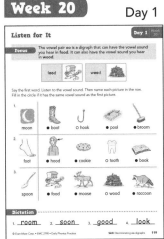

Listen for It — Day 1

Focus The vowel pair oo is a digraph that can have the vowel sound you hear in food. It can also have the vowel sound you hear in wood.
(food wood)

Say the first word. Listen to the vowel sound. Then name each picture in the row. Fill in the circle if it has the same vowel sound as the first picture.

1. moon   ● boot   ○ hook   ● pool   ● broom
2. foot   ● hood   ● cookie   ○ tooth   ● book
3. spoon   ● food   ● moose   ○ wood   ● raccoon

Dictation
1. room   2. soon   3. good   4. look

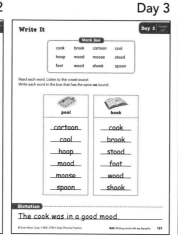
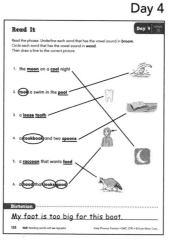
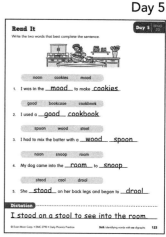

Day 2

Write It — Day 2 Week 20

Word Box

book cookie football hood hook broom
moose spoon raccoon tooth boot wood

Write the word that names the picture.

1. hook
2. cookie
3. raccoon
4. spoon
5. hood
6. moose
7. book
8. football
9. tooth
10. wood
11. broom
12. boot

Dictation

1. pool   2. food   3. moon   4. cook

120   Skill: Writing words with oo digraphs   Daily Phonics Practice • EMC 2790 • © Evan-Moor Corp.

Day 3

Write It — Day 3 Week 20

Word Box

cook brook cartoon cool
hoop mood moose stood
foot wood shook spoon

Read each word. Listen to the vowel sound.
Write each word in the box that has the same oo sound.

pool	book
cartoon	cook
cool	brook
hoop	stood
mood	foot
moose	wood
spoon	shook

Dictation

The cook was in a good mood.

© Evan-Moor Corp. • EMC 2790 • Daily Phonics Practice   121

Day 4

Read It — Day 4 Week 20

Read the phrase. Underline each word that has the vowel sound in broom.
Circle each word that has the vowel sound in wood.
Then draw a line to the correct picture.

1. the **moon** on a **cool** night
2. (took) a swim in the **pool**
3. a **loose tooth**
4. a (cookbook) and two **spoons**
5. a **raccoon** that wants **food**
6. a (hood) that (looks) (good)

Dictation

My foot is too big for this boot.

122   Skill: Reading words with oo digraphs   Daily Phonics Practice • EMC 2790 • © Evan-Moor Corp.

Day 5

Read It — Day 5 Week 20

Write the two words that best complete the sentence.

noon   cookies   mood
1. I was in the __mood__ to make __cookies__

good   bookcase   cookbook
2. I used a __good__ __cookbook__

spoon   wood   stool
3. I had to mix the batter with a __wood__ __spoon__

noon   snoop   room
4. My dog came into the __room__ to __snoop__

stood   cool   drool
5. She __stood__ on her back legs and began to __drool__

Dictation

I stood on a stool to see into the room.

© Evan-Moor Corp. • EMC 2790 • Daily Phonics Practice   123

Week 21

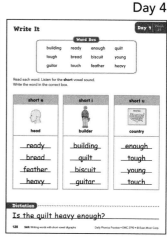

Day 1

Listen for It — Day 1 Week 21

Focus   The vowel digraph ea sometimes has the **short e** sound.

short e → head

Say the word. Do you hear the **short e** sound?
Fill in the circle next to **yes** or **no**.

1. bread — ●yes ○no
2. thread — ●yes ○no
3. peach — ○yes ●no
4. feather — ●yes ○no
5. sweater — ●yes ○no
6. eagle — ○yes ●no
7. breakfast — ●yes ○no
8. leaf — ○yes ●no
9. spread — ●yes ○no

Dictation

1. s w e a t   2. b r e a t h   3. d r e a d

© Evan-Moor Corp. • EMC 2790 • Daily Phonics Practice   Skill: Identifying short e digraphs   125

Day 2

Listen for It — Day 2 Week 21

Focus   The vowel pair ui is a digraph that can have the **short i** sound.
The vowel pair ou is a digraph that can have the **short u** sound.

short i → build   short u → country

Say the word. Listen for the **short i** or **short u** sound.
Underline the two letters that together have the **short i** or **short u** sound.

1. trouble
2. quilt
3. rough
4. double
5. couple
6. building
7. guitar
8. cousins
9. biscuit

Dictation

My cousin plays a guitar.

126   Skill: Identifying short i and short u digraphs   Daily Phonics Practice • EMC 2790 • © Evan-Moor Corp.

Day 3

Write It — Day 3 Week 21

Word Box

quilt double biscuit feather sweater building
bread guitar rough country trouble breakfast

Write the word that names the picture.

1. double
2. bread
3. quilt
4. sweater
5. building
6. trouble
7. biscuit
8. rough
9. feather
10. breakfast
11. guitar
12. country

Dictation

I had a biscuit for breakfast.

© Evan-Moor Corp. • EMC 2790 • Daily Phonics Practice   Skill: Writing words with short vowel digraphs   127

Day 4

Write It — Day 4 Week 21

Word Box

building ready enough quilt
tough bread biscuit young
guitar touch feather heavy

Read each word. Listen for the **short vowel** sound.
Write the word in the correct box.

short e	short i	short u
head	builder	country
ready	building	enough
bread	quilt	tough
feather	biscuit	young
heavy	guitar	touch

Dictation

Is the quilt heavy enough?

128   Skill: Writing words with short vowel digraphs   Daily Phonics Practice • EMC 2790 • © Evan-Moor Corp.

Day 5

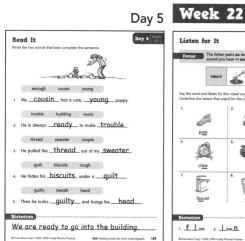

Read It — Day 5 Week 21

Write the two words that best complete the sentence.

enough   cousin   young
1. My __cousin__ has a cute, __young__ puppy.

trouble   building   ready
2. He is always __ready__ to make __trouble__

thread   sweater   couple
3. He pulled the __thread__ out of my __sweater__

quilt   biscuits   rough
4. He hides his __biscuits__ under a __quilt__

guilty   breath   head
5. Then he looks __guilty__ and hangs his __head__

Dictation

We are ready to go into the building.

© Evan-Moor Corp. • EMC 2790 • Daily Phonics Practice   Skill: Reading words with short vowel digraphs   129

Week 22

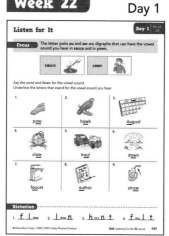

Day 1

Listen for It — Day 1 Week 22

Focus   The letter pairs au and aw are digraphs that can have the vowel
sound you hear in sauce and in yawn.

sauce   yawn

Say the word and listen for the vowel sound.
Underline the letters that stand for the vowel sound you hear.

1. paw
2. hawk
3. August
4. claw
5. haul
6. dawn
7. faucet
8. author
9. straw

Dictation

1. f l a w   2. l a w n   3. h a u n t   4. f a u l t

© Evan-Moor Corp. • EMC 2790 • Daily Phonics Practice   Skill: Listening for the /ô/ sound   131

Day 2

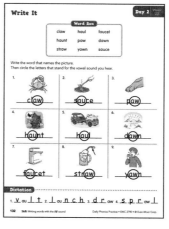

Write It — Day 2 Week 22

Word Box

claw haul faucet
haunt paw dawn
straw yawn sauce

Write the word that names the picture.
Then circle the letters that stand for the vowel sound you hear.

1. claw
2. sauce
3. paw
4. haunt
5. haul
6. dawn
7. faucet
8. straw
9. yawn

Dictation

1. v a u l t   2. l a u n c h   3. d r a w   4. s p r a w l

132   Skill: Writing words with the /ô/ sound   Daily Phonics Practice • EMC 2790 • © Evan-Moor Corp.

Day 3

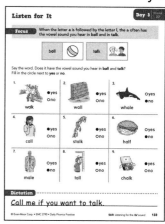

Listen for It — Day 3 Week 22

Focus   When the letter a is followed by the letter l, the a often has
the vowel sound you hear in ball and in talk.

ball   talk

Say the word. Does it have the vowel sound you hear in **ball** and **talk**?
Fill in the circle next to **yes** or **no**.

1. walk — ●yes ○no
2. wall — ●yes ○no
3. whale — ○yes ●no
4. call — ●yes ○no
5. stalk — ●yes ○no
6. half — ○yes ●no
7. male — ○yes ●no
8. tall — ●yes ○no
9. chalk — ●yes ○no

Dictation

Call me if you want to talk.

© Evan-Moor Corp. • EMC 2790 • Daily Phonics Practice   Skill: Listening for the /ô/ sound   133

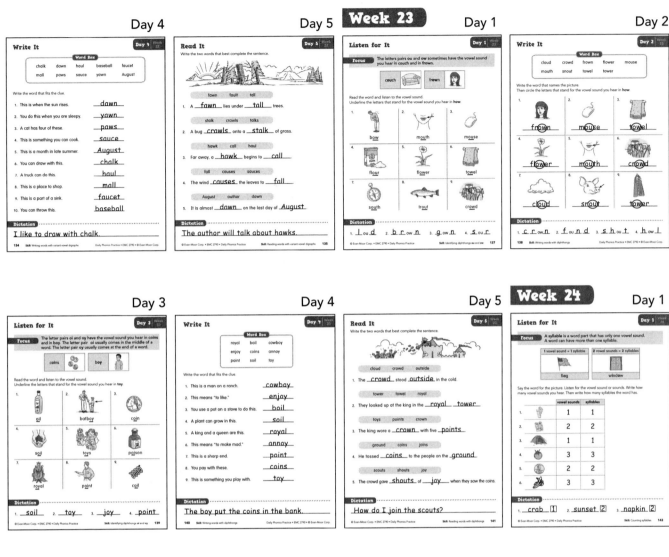

Write It — Day 4

Word Box: chalk, dawn, haul, baseball, faucet, mall, paws, sauce, yawn, August

Write the word that fits the clue.
1. This is when the sun rises. — dawn
2. You do this when you are sleepy. — yawn
3. A cat has four of these. — paws
4. This is something you can cook. — sauce
5. This is a month in late summer. — August
6. You can draw with this. — chalk
7. A truck can do this. — haul
8. This is a place to shop. — mall
9. This is a part of a sink. — faucet
10. You can throw this. — baseball

Dictation: I like to draw with chalk.

Read It — Day 5
Write the two words that best complete the sentence.
1. A **fawn** lies under **tall** trees.
2. A bug **crawls** onto a **stalk** of grass.
3. Far away, a **hawk** begins to **call**.
4. The wind **causes** the leaves to **fall**.
5. It is almost **dawn** on the last day of **August**.

Dictation: The author will talk about hawks.

Listen for It — Day 1
Focus: The letters pairs ou and ow sometimes have the vowel sound you hear in couch and in frown.
couch / frown

Read the word and listen to the vowel sound.
Underline the letters that stand for the vowel sound you hear in **how**.
1. bow 2. mouth 3. mouse
4. flour 5. flower 6. towel
7. south 8. trout 9. crowd

Dictation: 1. l_oud 2. br_own 3. g_own 4. s_our

Write It — Day 2
Word Box: cloud, crowd, frown, flower, mouse, mouth, snout, towel, tower

Write the word that names the picture.
Then circle the letters that stand for the vowel sound you hear in **how**.
1. frown 2. mouse 3. towel
4. flower 5. mouth 6. crowd
7. cloud 8. snout 9. tower

Dictation: 1. cr_own 2. f_ound 3. sh_out 4. h_owl

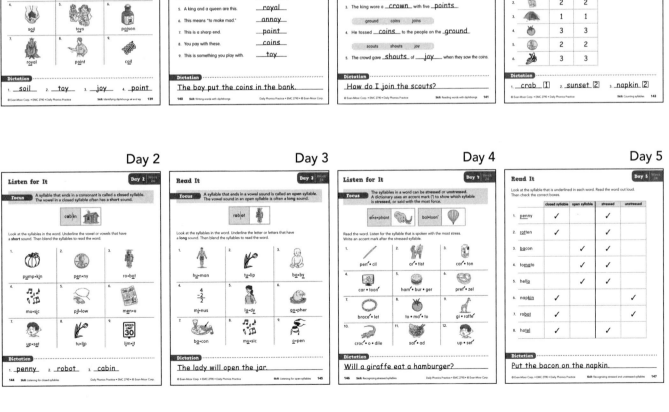

Listen for It — Day 3
Focus: The letter pairs oi and oy have the vowel sound you hear in coins and in boy. The letter pair oi usually comes in the middle of a word. The letter pair oy usually comes at the end of a word.
coins / boy

Read the word and listen to the vowel sound.
Underline the letters that stand for the vowel sound you hear in **toy**.
1. oil 2. batboy 3. coin
4. soil 5. toys 6. poison
7. royal 8. point 9. coil

Dictation: 1. soil 2. toy 3. joy 4. point

Write It — Day 4
Word Box: royal, boil, cowboy, enjoy, coins, annoy, point, soil, toy

Write the word that fits the clue.
1. This is a man on a ranch. — cowboy
2. This means "to like." — enjoy
3. You use a pot on a stove to do this. — boil
4. A plant can grow in this. — soil
5. A king and a queen are this. — royal
6. This means "to make mad." — annoy
7. This is a sharp end. — point
8. You pay with these. — coins
9. This is something you play with. — toy

Dictation: The boy put the coins in the bank.

Read It — Day 5
Write the two words that best complete the sentence.
1. The **crowd** stood **outside** in the cold.
2. They looked up at the king in the **royal** **tower**.
3. The king wore a **crown** with five **points**.
4. He tossed **coins** to the people on the **ground**.
5. The crowd gave **shouts** of **joy** when they saw the coins.

Dictation: How do I join the scouts?

Listen for It — Day 1
Focus: A syllable is a word part that has only one vowel sound. A word can have more than one syllable.
1 vowel sound = 1 syllable / 2 vowel sounds = 2 syllables
flag / window

Say the word for the picture. Listen for the vowel sound or sounds. Write how many vowel sounds you hear. Then write how many syllables the word has.

	vowel sounds	syllables
1	1	1
2	2	2
3	1	1
4	3	3
5	2	2
6	3	3

Dictation: 1. crab [1] 2. sunset [2] 3. napkin [2]

Listen for It — Day 2
Focus: A syllable that ends in a consonant is called a closed syllable. The vowel in a closed syllable often has a short sound.
cab•in

Look at the syllables in the word. Underline the vowel or vowels that have a short sound. Then blend the syllables to read the word.
1. pump•kin 2. pen•ny 3. ro•bot
4. mu•sic 5. pil•low 6. men•u
7. up•set 8. tu•lip 9. lim•it

Dictation: 1. penny 2. robot 3. cabin

Read It — Day 3
Focus: A syllable that ends in a vowel sound is called an open syllable. The vowel sound in an open syllable is often a long sound.
ro•bot

Look at the syllables in the word. Underline the letter or letters that have a long sound. Then blend the syllables to read the word.
1. hu•man 2. tu•lip 3. ba•by
4. mi•nus 5. la•dy 6. go•pher
7. ba•con 8. mu•sic 9. o•pen

Dictation: The lady will open the jar.

Listen for It — Day 4
Focus: The syllables in a word can be stressed or unstressed. A dictionary uses an accent mark (') to show which syllable is stressed, or said with the most force.
el•e•phant / bal•loon'

Read the word. Listen for the syllable that is spoken with the most stress. Write an accent mark after the stressed syllable.
1. pen'•cil 2. ar'•tist 3. car•ton
4. car•toon' 5. ham'•bur•ger 6. pret'•zel
7. brace'•let 8. to•ma'•to 9. gi•raffe'
10. croc'•o•dile 11. sal'•ad 12. up•set'

Dictation: Will a giraffe eat a hamburger?

Read It — Day 5
Look at the syllable that is underlined in each word. Read the word out loud. Then check the correct boxes.

	closed syllable	open syllable	stressed	unstressed
1. penny	✓		✓	
2. rotten	✓		✓	
3. bacon		✓	✓	
4. tomato		✓	✓	
5. hello		✓	✓	
6. napkin	✓			✓
7. robot	✓			✓
8. hotel	✓		✓	

Dictation: Put the bacon on the napkin.

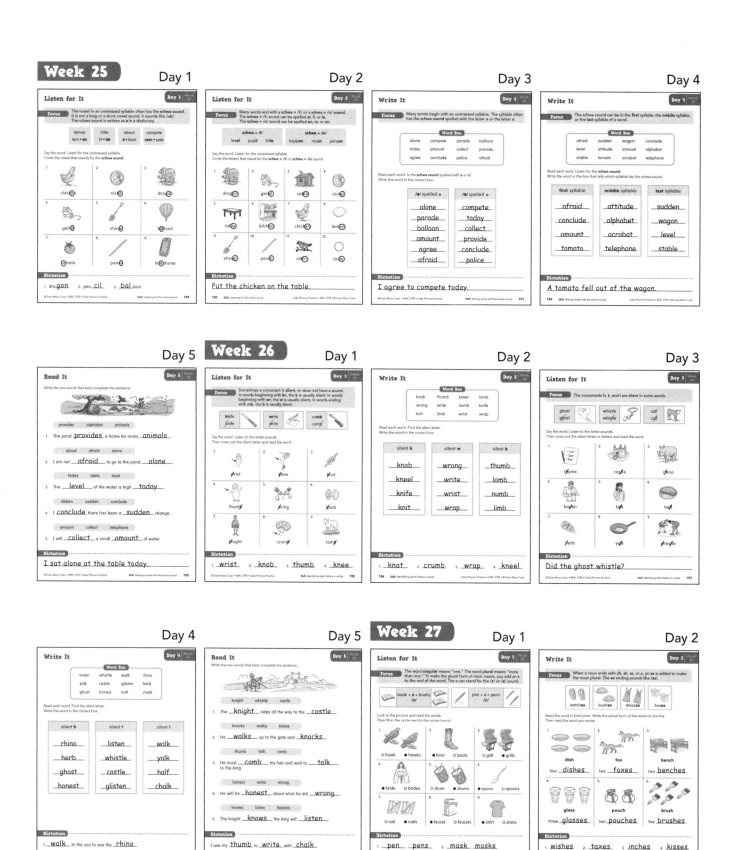

Week 25

Day 1

Listen for It — Day 1, Week 25

Focus The vowel in an unstressed syllable often has the schwa sound. It is not a long or a short vowel sound. It sounds like /uh/. The schwa sound is written as ə in a dictionary.

lemon	little	about	compete
lem • ən	lit • təl	ə • bout	com • pete

Say the word. Listen for the unstressed syllable.
Circle the vowel that stands for the schwa sound.

1. chicken   2. nickel   3. dragon
4. gerbil   5. shovel   6. balloon
7. tomato   8. pencil   9. telephone

Dictation
1. dra**gon**   2. pen**cil**   3. **bal**loon

Day 2

Listen for It — Day 2, Week 25

Focus Many words end with a schwa + /l/ or a schwa + /n/ sound. The schwa + /l/ sound can be spelled el, il, or le. The schwa + /n/ sound can be spelled en, in, or on.

schwa + /l/		schwa + /n/	
level	little	happen	person
pupil		raisin	

Say the word. Listen for the unstressed syllable.
Circle the letters that stand for the schwa + /l/ or schwa + /n/ sound.

1. dragon   2. gerbil   3. cabin   4. nickel
5. table   6. kitchen   7. chicken   8. lemon
9. shovel   10. pencil   11. raisin   12. circle

Dictation
Put the chicken on the table.

Day 3

Write It — Day 3, Week 25

Focus Many words begin with an unstressed syllable. The syllable often has the schwa sound spelled with the letter a or the letter o.

Word Box

alone	compete	parade	balloon
today	amount	collect	provide
agree	conclude	police	afraid

Read each word. Is the schwa sound spelled with a or o?
Write the word in the correct box.

/ə/ spelled a	/ə/ spelled o
alone	compete
parade	today
balloon	collect
amount	provide
agree	conclude
afraid	police

Dictation
I agree to compete today.

Day 4

Write It — Day 4, Week 25

Focus The schwa sound can be in the first syllable, the middle syllable, or the last syllable of a word.

Word Box

afraid	sudden	wagon	conclude
level	attitude	amount	alphabet
stable	tomato	acrobat	telephone

Read each word. Listen for the schwa sound.
Write the word in the box that tells which syllable has the schwa sound.

first syllable	middle syllable	last syllable
afraid	attitude	sudden
conclude	alphabet	wagon
amount	acrobat	level
tomato	telephone	stable

Dictation
A tomato fell out of the wagon.

Day 5

Read It — Day 5, Week 25

Write the two words that best complete the sentence.

provides	alphabet	animals

1. The pond **provides** a home for many **animals**.

aloud	afraid	alone

2. I am not **afraid** to go to the pond **alone**.

today	table	level

3. The **level** of the water is high **today**.

ribbon	sudden	conclude

4. I **conclude** there has been a **sudden** change.

amount	collect	telephone

5. I will **collect** a small **amount** of water.

Dictation
I sat alone at the table today.

Week 26

Day 1

Listen for It — Day 1, Week 26

Focus Sometimes a consonant is silent, or does not have a sound. In words beginning with kn, the k is usually silent. In words beginning with wr, the w is usually silent. In words ending with mb, the b is usually silent.

knife	write	comb

Say the word. Listen to the letter-sounds.
Then cross out the silent letter and read the word.

1. wrist   2. knee   3. knot
4. thumb   5. wring   6. knob
7. knight   8. crumb   9. lamb

Dictation
1. wrist   2. knob   3. thumb   4. knee

Day 2

Write It — Day 2, Week 26

Word Box

knob	thumb	kneel	lamb
wrong	write	numb	knife
knit	limb	wrist	wrap

Read each word. Find the silent letter.
Write the word in the correct box.

silent k	silent w	silent b
knob	wrong	thumb
kneel	write	lamb
knife	wrist	numb
knit	wrap	limb

Dictation
1. knot   2. crumb   3. wrap   4. kneel

Day 3

Listen for It — Day 3, Week 26

Focus The consonants h, t, and l are silent in some words.

ghost	whistle	calf

Say the word. Listen to the letter-sounds.
Then cross out the silent letter or letters and read the word.

1. rhyme   2. castle   3. rhino
4. fasten   5. talk   6. half
7. herb   8. yolk   9. wrestle

Dictation
Did the ghost whistle?

Day 4

Write It — Day 4, Week 26

Word Box

listen	whistle	walk	rhino
yolk	castle	glisten	herb
ghost	honest	half	chalk

Read each word. Find the silent letter.
Write the word in the correct box.

silent h	silent t	silent l
rhino	listen	walk
herb	whistle	yolk
ghost	castle	half
honest	glisten	chalk

Dictation
1. walk to the zoo to see the rhino.

Day 5

Read It — Day 5, Week 26

Write the two words that best complete the sentence.

knight	whistle	castle

1. The **knight** rides all the way to the **castle**.

knocks	walks	knees

2. He **walks** up to the gate and **knocks**.

thumb	talk	comb

3. He must **comb** his hair and wait to **talk** to the king.

honest	write	wrong

4. He will be **honest** about what he did **wrong**.

knows	listen	fastens

5. The knight **knows** the king will **listen**.

Dictation
I use my thumb to write with chalk.

Week 27

Day 1

Listen for It — Day 1, Week 27

Focus The word **singular** means "one." The word **plural** means "more than one." To make the plural form of most nouns, you add an s to the end of the word. The s can stand for the /s/ or /z/ sound.

book + s = books	pen + s = pens
/s/	/z/

Look at the picture and read the words.
Then fill in the circle next to the correct word.

1. ○ hawk   ● hawks
2. ○ boot   ● boots
3. ○ grill   ● grills
4. ● bride   ○ brides
5. ○ drum   ● drums
6. ○ spoon   ○ spoons
7. ○ nail   ● nails
8. ● faucet   ○ faucets
9. ○ shirt   ● shirts

Dictation
1. pen   pens   2. mask   masks

Day 2

Write It — Day 2, Week 27

Focus When a noun ends with ch, sh, ss, or x, an es is added to make the noun plural. The es ending sounds like /əz/.

watches	bushes	dresses	boxes

Read the word in bold print. Write the plural form of the word on the line.
Then read the word you wrote.

1. dish — four **dishes**
2. fox — two **foxes**
3. bench — two **benches**
4. glass — three **glasses**
5. pouch — two **pouches**
6. brush — five **brushes**

Dictation
1. wishes   2. taxes   3. inches   4. kisses

Day 3

Write It — Day 3 Week 27

Focus When a noun ends with the letter f, the plural form is made by changing the f to a v and adding es.

loaf f + es = loaves

Read the word in bold print. Write the plural form of the word on the line. Then read the word you wrote.

1. leaf — three leaves
2. wolf — three wolves
3. half — two halves
4. knife — five knives
5. calf — two calves
6. scarf — two scarves

Dictation
1. life lives
2. shelf shelves

© Evan-Moor Corp. • EMC 2790 • Daily Phonics Practice   Skill: Writing plural nouns   163

Day 4

Write It — Day 3 Week 27

Focus When a noun ends with a y that follows a consonant, the plural form of the noun is made by changing the y to i and adding es. The s sounds like /z/.

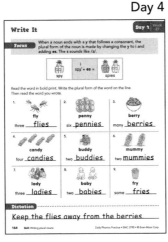

spy y + es = spies

Read the word in bold print. Write the plural form of the word on the line. Then read the word you wrote.

1. fly — three flies
2. penny — six pennies
3. berry — many berries
4. candy — four candies
5. buddy — two buddies
6. mummy — two mummies
7. lady — three ladies
8. baby — two babies
9. fry — some fries

Dictation
Keep the flies away from the berries.

164   Skill: Writing plural nouns   Daily Phonics Practice • EMC 2790 • © Evan-Moor Corp.

Day 5

Read It — Day 5 Week 27

Write the two words that best complete the sentence.

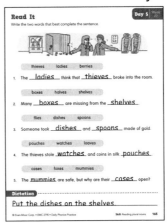

1. thieves | ladies | berries
   The ladies think that thieves broke into the room.
2. boxes | halves | shelves
   Many boxes are missing from the shelves.
3. flies | dishes | spoons
   Someone took dishes and spoons made of gold.
4. pouches | watches | loaves
   The thieves stole watches and coins in silk pouches.
5. cases | foxes | mummies
   The mummies are safe, but why are their cases open?

Dictation
Put the dishes on the shelves.

© Evan-Moor Corp. • EMC 2790 • Daily Phonics Practice   Skill: Reading plural nouns   165

Week 28 — Day 1

Listen for It — Day 1 Week 28

Focus Some plural forms of nouns are very different from their singular forms. The vowels might change, or the whole word might change.

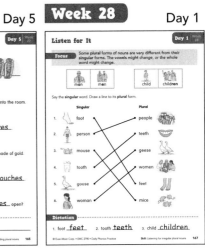

man — men   child — children

Say the singular word. Draw a line to its plural form.

Singular	Plural
1. foot	people
2. person	teeth
3. mouse	geese
4. tooth	women
5. goose	feet
6. woman	mice

Dictation
1. foot feet
2. tooth teeth
3. child children

© Evan-Moor Corp. • EMC 2790 • Daily Phonics Practice   Skill: Listening for irregular plural nouns   167

Day 2

Write It — Day 2 Week 28

Word Box

feet	mouse	geese	foot
child	teeth	woman	children
women	mice	tooth	goose

Read each word. Write the word in the correct box.

singular one	plural more than one
foot	feet
mouse	mice
goose	geese
child	children
tooth	teeth
woman	women

Dictation
The mice ran away from the men.

168   Skill: Writing irregular plural nouns   Daily Phonics Practice • EMC 2790 • © Evan-Moor Corp.

Day 3

Write It — Day 3 Week 28

Focus Some nouns have the same singular and plural forms.

fish — fish   jeans — jeans

Read the first phrase in each row. Underline the singular noun. Then write the plural form of the noun to complete the second phrase.

1. one moose — a herd of moose
2. a pair of pants — two pairs of pants
3. one sheep — a flock of sheep
4. this deer — those deer
5. my glasses — two cases of glasses
6. one pair of shorts — two pairs of shorts
7. one pair of scissors — some scissors

Dictation
1. jeans
2. sheep
3. shorts
4. moose

© Evan-Moor Corp. • EMC 2790 • Daily Phonics Practice   Skill: Writing irregular plural nouns   169

Day 4

Write It — Day 4 Week 28

Word Box

glasses	moose	feet	women	mice
scissors	pants	geese	teeth	men

Write the word that fits the clue.

1. These animals can fly. — geese
2. These animals are very big. — moose
3. You cut with these. — scissors
4. You chew with these. — teeth
5. These people are not men. — women
6. You pull these over your legs. — pants
7. These help you see. — glasses
8. You stand on these. — feet
9. These people are not women. — men
10. These animals are very small. — mice

Dictation
The women have the same glasses.

170   Skill: Writing irregular plural nouns   Daily Phonics Practice • EMC 2790 • © Evan-Moor Corp.

Day 5

Read It — Day 5 Week 28

Write the two words that best complete the sentence.

1. sheep | sheeps | geese
   Two sheep went to the pond to find some geese.
2. meese | children | mice
   The geese had gone to see two tiny mice and their young children.
3. feet | glasses | glass
   One sheep lost its glasses fell in, and got its feet wet.
4. fish | tooths | teeth
   A bunch of fish bit the sheep with their teeth.
5. people | pantses | pants
   The sheep wished it wore pants like people do!

Dictation
I saw six fish and three geese.

© Evan-Moor Corp. • EMC 2790 • Daily Phonics Practice   Skill: Reading irregular plural nouns   171

Week 29 — Day 1

Write It — Day 1 Week 29

Focus Most verbs are action words. When a verb ends with ed, it means the action has already happened. When a verb ends with ing, it means the action is or was in the process of happening.

action	+ ed	+ ing
I paint.	I painted last week.	I am painting now. I was painting before.

Read the word. Then write it with each ending. Read the new words you wrote. Listen for the sound that ed has in each word.

action (base word)	+ ed	+ ing
1. pack	packed	packing
2. turn	turned	turning
3. open	opened	opening
4. talk	talked	talking
5. visit	visited	visiting
6. rain	rained	raining
7. print	printed	printing
8. listen	listened	listening

Dictation
1. walking
2. folded
3. mixed
4. helping

© Evan-Moor Corp. • EMC 2790 • Daily Phonics Practice   Skill: Writing verbs with inflectional endings   173

Day 2

Write It — Day 2 Week 29

Focus When a verb ends in a silent e, you drop the e before adding the ed or ing ending.

action	+ ed	+ ing
I skate.	I skated last week.	I am skating now. I was skating before.

Read the base word. Then follow the rule to add ed to the base word. Follow the rule again to add ing to the base word.

action (base word)	+ ed	+ ing
1. save	saved	saving
2. joke	joked	joking
3. like	liked	liking
4. hope	hoped	hoping
5. trade	traded	trading
6. chase	chased	chasing
7. serve	served	serving
8. decide	decided	deciding

Dictation
1. waved
2. waving
3. biked
4. biking

174   Skill: Writing verbs with inflectional endings   Daily Phonics Practice • EMC 2790 • © Evan-Moor Corp.

Day 3

Write It — Day 3 Week 29

Focus When a verb ends with a consonant after a short vowel sound, the final consonant is doubled before ed or ing is added.

action	double the consonant and add ed	double the consonant and add ing
I shop.	I shopped last week.	I am shopping now. I was shopping before.

Read the base word. Then follow the rule to add ed to the base word. Follow the rule again to add ing to the base word.

action (base word)	+ ed	+ ing
1. zip	zipped	zipping
2. clap	clapped	clapping
3. brag	bragged	bragging
4. chat	chatted	chatting
5. grin	grinned	grinning
6. plan	planned	planning
7. shred	shredded	shredding
8. scrub	scrubbed	scrubbing

Dictation
1. slipped
2. slipping
3. added
4. adding

© Evan-Moor Corp. • EMC 2790 • Daily Phonics Practice   Skill: Writing verbs with inflectional endings   175

Day 4

Write It — Day 4 Week 29

Focus Sometimes a verb has an s or an es at the end. This ending shows that only one person or thing is or was doing the action. An s is added to verbs that end in a consonant or a silent e. An es is added to verbs that end in ch, sh, ss, or x.

paint	skate	teach	wash	toss	fix
paints	skates	teaches	washes	tosses	fixes

Read the verb. Follow the rule to add s or es.

1. pass — passes	2. mix — mixes	3. match — matches
4. begin — begins	5. finish — finishes	6. relax — relaxes
7. reach — reaches	8. guess — guesses	9. brush — brushes
10. smile — smiles	11. join — joins	12. dress — dresses

Dictation
1. The test begins.
2. She smiles and relaxes.

176   Skill: Writing verbs with plural endings   Daily Phonics Practice • EMC 2790 • © Evan-Moor Corp.

© Evan-Moor Corp. • EMC 2790 • Daily Phonics   **207**

Week 30 — Day 5 — Read It

Write the two words that best complete the sentence.

1. scored / scarred / kicked — Lucas __kicked__ the ball and almost __scored__ a goal.
2. rolling / stooped / stopped — The ball was __rolling__ into the net, but Sam __stopped__ it.
3. jumping / clipped / clapping — The crowd was __clapping__ and __jumping__ up and down.
4. reaches / diving / driving — Sam always __reaches__ the ball by __diving__ just in time.
5. washed / wishes / likes — Lucas __likes__ Sam and __wishes__ Sam was on his team.

Dictation

Mom likes to take me shopping.

© Evan-Moor Corp. • EMC 2790 • Daily Phonics Practice   Skill: Reading verbs with inflectional endings   177

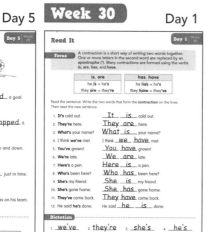

Week 30 — Day 1 — Read It

Focus: A contraction is a short way of writing two words together. One or more letters in the second word are replaced by an apostrophe ('). Many contractions are formed using the verbs is, are, has, and have.

is, are	has, have
he is = he's	has, have
they are = they're	they have = they've

Read the sentence. Write the two words that form the contraction on the lines. Then read the new sentence.

1. It's cold out. — __It is__ cold out.
2. They're here. — __They are__ here.
3. What's your name? — __What is__ your name?
4. I think we've met. — I think __we have__ met.
5. You've grown! — __You have__ grown!
6. We're late. — __We are__ late.
7. Here's a pen. — __Here is__ a pen.
8. Who's been here? — __Who has__ been here?
9. She's my friend. — __She is__ my friend.
10. She's gone home. — __She has__ gone home.
11. They've come back. — __They have__ come back.
12. He said he's done. — He said __he is__ done.

Dictation

1. we've 2. they're 3. she's 4. he's

© Evan-Moor Corp. • EMC 2790 • Daily Phonics Practice   Skill: Writing and reading contractions   179

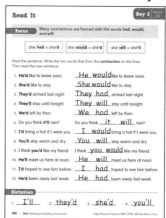

Week 30 — Day 2 — Read It

Focus: Many contractions are formed with the words had, would, and will.

she had = she'd	she would = she'd	she will = she'll

Read the sentence. Write the two words that form the contraction on the lines. Then read the new sentence.

1. He'd like to leave soon. — __He would__ like to leave soon.
2. She'd like to stay. — __She would__ like to stay.
3. They'd arrived last night. — __They had__ arrived last night.
4. They'll stay until tonight. — __They will__ stay until tonight.
5. We'd left by then. — __We had__ left by then.
6. Do you think it'll rain? — Do you think __it will__ rain?
7. I'd bring a hat if I were you. — __I would__ bring a hat if I were you.
8. You'll stay warm and dry. — __You will__ stay warm and dry.
9. I think you'd like my friend. — I think __you would__ like my friend.
10. He'll meet us here at noon. — __He will__ meet us here at noon.
11. I'd hoped to see him before. — __I had__ hoped to see him before.
12. He'd been away last week. — __He had__ been away last week.

Dictation

1. I'll 2. they'd 3. she'd 4. you'll

180   Skill: Writing and reading contractions   Daily Phonics Practice • EMC 2790 • © Evan-Moor Corp.

Week 30 — Day 3 — Read It

Focus: Many contractions are formed with the word not.

does not = doesn't	is not = isn't	do not = don't	will not = won't

Read the phrase. Fill in the circle next to the contraction that stands for the bold words.

1. she was not — ● wasn't ○ weren't
2. they did not — ● don't ○ didn't
3. he could not — ● couldn't ○ can't
4. we will not — ● won't ○ wouldn't
5. it is not — ○ doesn't ● isn't
6. you have not — ● haven't ○ hasn't
7. they are not — ○ isn't ● aren't
8. I should not — ○ won't ● shouldn't
9. you were not — ● weren't ○ won't
10. she has not — ● hasn't ○ wasn't
11. I cannot — ● couldn't ○ can't
12. he does not — ● doesn't ○ can't

Dictation

You shouldn't go if you aren't well.

© Evan-Moor Corp. • EMC 2790 • Daily Phonics Practice   Skill: Writing and reading contractions   181

Week 30 — Day 4 — Write It

Read the two words. Write their contraction on the line.

1. who is — who's
2. you are — you're
3. he has — he's
4. is not — isn't
5. they would — they'd
6. I have — I've
7. we will — we'll
8. I had — I'd
9. does not — doesn't
10. should have — should've
11. could not — couldn't
12. they are — they're
13. what is — what's
14. she has — she's
15. there would — there'd

Dictation

He'll find out if they're here.

182   Skill: Writing and reading contractions   Daily Phonics Practice • EMC 2790 • © Evan-Moor Corp.

Week 30 — Day 5 — Read It

Write the two words that best complete the sentence.

1. Weren't / We're / We've — __We're__ glad that __you've__ come to visit us.
2. you'd / We'll / We'd — __We'd__ hoped that __you'd__ be here by now.
3. they've / I'll / you're — __I'll__ unpack the car if __you're__ too tired.
4. it's / can't / isn't — I __can't__ believe __it's__ been a year since we saw you!
5. would've / shouldn't / couldn't — We __would've__ gone to see you, but we __couldn't__.

Dictation

This isn't where we'll stay.

© Evan-Moor Corp. • EMC 2790 • Daily Phonics Practice   Skill: Writing and reading contractions   183

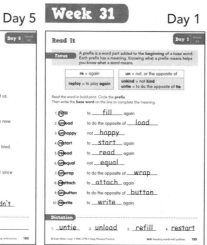

Week 31 — Day 1 — Read It

Focus: A prefix is a word part added to the beginning of a base word. Each prefix has a meaning. Knowing what a prefix means helps you know what a word means.

re = again	un = not, or the opposite of
replay = to play again	unkind = not kind / untie = to do the opposite of tie

Read the word in bold print. Circle the prefix. Then write the base word on the line to complete the meaning.

1. refill — to __fill__ again
2. unload — to do the opposite of __load__
3. unhappy — not __happy__
4. restart — to __start__ again
5. reread — to __read__ again
6. unequal — not __equal__
7. unwrap — to do the opposite of __wrap__
8. reattach — to __attach__ again
9. unbutton — to do the opposite of __button__
10. rewrite — to __write__ again

Dictation

1. untie 2. unload 3. refill 4. restart

© Evan-Moor Corp. • EMC 2790 • Daily Phonics Practice   Skill: Reading words with prefixes   185

Week 31 — Day 2 — Write It

Focus: Each prefix has a meaning. Knowing what a prefix means helps you know what a word means.

re = again	un = not, or the opposite of

unlucky · retie · uneven · rewrap · uncover
reheat · unzip · unfair · rebuild · unpack

Write the word from above that matches the meaning.

1. to heat again — reheat
2. not even — uneven
3. to wrap again — rewrap
4. to do the opposite of pack — unpack
5. not fair — unfair
6. not lucky — unlucky
7. to tie again — retie
8. to do the opposite of zip — unzip
9. to build again — rebuild
10. to do the opposite of cover — uncover

Dictation

They will rebuild the uneven road.

186   Skill: Writing words with prefixes   Daily Phonics Practice • EMC 2790 • © Evan-Moor Corp.

Week 31 — Day 3 — Read It

Focus:
mis = incorrectly, or badly	dis = not, or the opposite of
misread = to read incorrectly	dislike = to not like / displease = to do the opposite of please

Read the word in bold print. Circle the prefix. Then write the base word on the line to complete the meaning.

1. distrust — to not __trust__
2. disagree — to not __agree__
3. misspell — to __spell__ incorrectly
4. disconnect — to do the opposite of __connect__
5. mistreat — to __treat__ badly
6. mislead — to __lead__ incorrectly
7. disappear — to do the opposite of __appear__
8. disrespect — to not __respect__
9. misspeak — to __speak__ incorrectly
10. misbehave — to __behave__ badly

Dictation

I distrust you because you misbehave.

© Evan-Moor Corp. • EMC 2790 • Daily Phonics Practice   Skill: Reading words with prefixes   187

Week 31 — Day 4 — Write It

Focus: Each prefix has a meaning. Knowing what a prefix means helps you know what a word means.

mis = incorrectly, or badly	dis = the opposite of

disagree · mistreat · dishonest · disconnect · misunderstand
miscount · misjudge · disrespect · disappear · mislead

Write the word from above that matches the meaning.

1. to treat badly — mistreat
2. to count incorrectly — miscount
3. the opposite of respect — disrespect
4. to do the opposite of agree — disagree
5. to judge incorrectly — misjudge
6. to do the opposite of connect — disconnect
7. to understand incorrectly — misunderstand
8. to be the opposite of honest — dishonest
9. to do the opposite of appear — disappear
10. to lead incorrectly — mislead

Dictation

Do not be dishonest or mislead me.

188   Skill: Writing words with prefixes   Daily Phonics Practice • EMC 2790 • © Evan-Moor Corp.

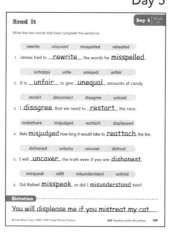

Week 31 — Day 5 — Read It

Write the two words that best complete the sentence.

1. rewrite / miscount / misspelled / reheated — James had to __rewrite__ the words he __misspelled__.
2. unhappy / untie / unequal / unfair — It is __unfair__ to give __unequal__ amounts of candy.
3. restart / disconnect / disagree / unload — I __disagree__ that we need to __restart__ the race.
4. misbehave / misjudged / reattach / displeased — Bela __misjudged__ how long it would take to __reattach__ the tire.
5. dishonest / unlucky / uncover / distrust — I will __uncover__ the truth even if you are __dishonest__.
6. misspeak / refill / misunderstand / unkind — Did Rafael __misspeak__ or did I __misunderstand__ him?

Dictation

You will displease me if you mistreat my cat.

© Evan-Moor Corp. • EMC 2790 • Daily Phonics Practice   Skill: Reading words with prefixes   189

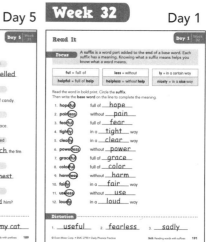

Week 32 — Day 1 — Read It

Focus: A suffix is a word part added to the end of a base word. Each suffix has a meaning. Knowing what a suffix means helps you know what a word means.

ful = full of	less = without	ly = in a certain way
helpful = full of help	helpless = without help	nicely = in a nice way

Read the word in bold print. Circle the suffix. Then write the base word on the line to complete the meaning.

1. hopeful — full of __hope__
2. painless — without __pain__
3. fearful — full of __fear__
4. tightly — in a __tight__ way
5. clearly — in a __clear__ way
6. powerless — without __power__
7. graceful — full of __grace__
8. colorful — full of __color__
9. harmless — without __harm__
10. fairly — in a __fair__ way
11. useless — without __use__
12. loudly — in a __loud__ way

Dictation

1. useful 2. fearless 3. sadly

© Evan-Moor Corp. • EMC 2790 • Daily Phonics Practice   Skill: Reading words with suffixes   191